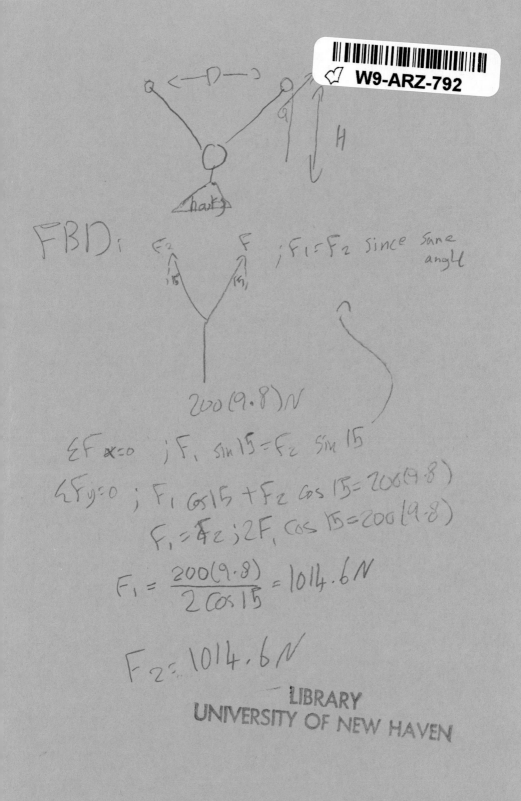

FBD: F_2 F ; $F_1 = F_2$ since same angle

$200(9.8)N$

$\Sigma F_x = 0$; $F_1 \sin 15 = F_2 \sin 15$

$\Sigma F_y = 0$; $F_1 \cos 15 + F_2 \cos 15 = 200(9.8)$

$F_1 = F_2$; $2F_1 \cos 15 = 200(9.8)$

$F_1 = \dfrac{200(9.8)}{2 \cos 15} = 1014.6 N$

$F_2 = 1014.6 N$

FBD:

F_2 F_p since same angles

$200(9.8)N$

$\Sigma F_x = 0$; $F_1 \sin 15 = F_2 \sin 15$

$\Sigma F_y = 0$; $F_1 \cos 15 + F_2 \cos 15 = 200(9.8)N$

$F_1 = F_2$; $2F_1 \cos 15 = 200(9.8)N$

$F_1 = \dfrac{200(9.8)}{2\cos 15} = 1014.6 N$

$F_2 = 1014.6 N$

I : assume numbers are in cell $A_1 : A_4$

= Max($A_1 : A_4$)

J : assume cell that has $\bar{a}$ is A_1

= Convert (A_1 "c" ; "F")

K : assume cell that has $\check{c}$ is A_1

= Convert (A_1 "c" ; "K")

CG : $S_2(0.99) = S_4(0.8)$ $S_2(0.01) = \frac{1}{4}(0.004)$
$+ S_3(0.004)$

Education's Lasting Influence on Values

① CG₁

$$S_2(0.99) = S_4(0.8)$$

$$S_2(0.99) - S_4(0.8) = 0$$

$$S_2(0.99) = S_4(0.8)$$

$$S_2(0.99) - S_4(0.8) = 0$$

② CS₁ $S_1 = S_4(0.196) + S_3$

$$S_2(0.01) = S_4(0.004) + S_3(0.004)$$

$$S_2(0.01) - S_4(0.004) - S_3(0.004) = 0$$

③

w

$$S_1 = S_4(0.196) + S_3$$

$$S_1 - S_4(0.196) - S_3 = 0$$

④ overall

$$S_1 + S_2 - S_3 - S_4 = 0$$

CG:

$$S_2(0.99) = S_4(0.8)$$

$$S_2(0.99) - S_4(0.8) \leq 0$$

CG:

$$S_2(0.99) = S_4(0.8)$$

$$S_2(0.99) - S_4(0.8) = 0$$

CS:

$$S_2(0.01) = S_4(0.004) + S_3(0.004)$$

$$S_2(0.01) - S_4(0.004) - S_3(0.004) \leq 0$$

$$S_1 = S_4(0.196) + S_8$$

$$S_1 - S_4(0.196) - S_3$$

Education's Lasting Influence on Values

Herbert H. Hyman & Charles R. Wright

$$S_2(0.01) = S_4(0.004) + S_3(0.004)$$

$$S_1 = S_4(0.196) + S_3$$

$$S_1 - S_4(0.196) - S_3 = 0$$

Overall

$$S_1 + S_2 - S_3 - S_4 = 0$$

The University of Chicago Press
Chicago & London

The University of Chicago Press, Chicago 60637
The University of Chicago Press, Ltd., London

Library of Congress Cataloging in Publication Data

Hyman, Herbert Hiram, 1918–
    Education's lasting influence on values.

    Includes index.
    1.   Education—United States—aims and objectives.
2.   Moral education—United States.   I.   Wright,
Charles Robert, 1927–   II.   Title.
        LA210.H93   370.11′0973   78-23376
ISBN 0-226-36542-5

$$a) V = ? \quad \alpha = V_{\omega} t \; ; \; V_{0x} = V \cos 45°$$

$$B)$$

LA
210
H93

$$B) y = y_1 + V_{0y} t - \tfrac{1}{2} g t^2$$

HERBERT H. HYMAN is the Crowell University Professor
of Social Sciences at Wesleyan University. CHARLES
R. WRIGHT is professor of communications at the
Annenberg School of Communications at the University
of Pennsylvania.

$$= Find(" ", Al, Find(" ", Al) + 2)$$

$$= find(" ", Al, Find(" ", Al) + 3)$$

$$= find(":", Al, Find(":", Al))$$

$$= find(":", Al, Find(":", Al) + 1)$$

$$= left(Al, Find(" ", Al, 1) - 1)$$

$$= left(Al, Find(" ", Al, 3) - 1) - (Al, find(" ", Al, 1) - 1)$$

$$= left(Al, Find(" ", Ai, 4) - 1) - left(Al, Find(" ", Al, 3) - 1)$$

$$= find(" ", Al, Find(" ", Al) + 2)$$

$$left(Al, Find(" ", Al, 1) - 1)$$

a) $V = ?$ $x = V_0 \alpha t$; $V_{0\alpha} = V\cos 45°$

$x = V(\cos 45) t$; $V = \dfrac{x}{(\cos 45)(4)} =$

$\dfrac{70\sqrt{2}}{\cos 45 (3 s)} = 33 \, \sqrt{5} \, \text{m/s}$

B) $y_2 = y_1 + V_{0y} t - \dfrac{1}{2} g t^2$

$10 = 4 + $

Contents

•

Acknowledgments

We express our appreciation to the Spencer Foundation and to its president, Dr. H. Thomas James, for the continuing generous support and encouragement of our studies on the enduring effects of education.

John Shelton Reed, our collaborator and co-author in the first study, gave continuing help in the design of the current study and made valuable suggestions for the analysis and report, though he bears no responsibility for any faults that may remain.

The sample surveys available in archives were the scientific wealth we continued to tap for our studies. We thank the National Opinion Research Center and its librarian, Patrick Bova, and the Roper Public Opinion Research Center and its director, Philip K. Hastings, for their cooperation in making their data available.

We express our debt to the Computer Center of Wesleyan University for efficiently processing a large volume of data and to Jon Spector, who rendered fine services as programmer throughout the current study.

For carrying the burdens of typing a lengthy manuscript, once again we thank Irene Spinnler for continuing to work in so congenial and careful a fashion.

1 Introduction

In 1975 we presented substantial evidence that education increases knowledge, deepens receptivity to further knowledge, and stimulates active seeking for new information in American adults long after they finish their formal schooling.[1] A novel method, applied to data that were available in abundance but had been neglected by educational researchers, yielded evidence on about 80,000 white adults of all ages from twenty-five to seventy-two. These data came from many national samples representative of students taught in all American schools and colleges during several historical periods, who had reached various levels of educational attainment and had been molded by the differing environments in which they learned, matured, and grew old. We have now applied that same method to another extensive but neglected set of data drawn from many national samples to provide generalizable evidence on the enduring effects of education on values. Even if education accomplished nothing else, the large and lasting changes it brings in the cognitive realm surely are a major achievement; but exploring its enduring effects in the realm of values takes us closer to our goal of testing the full claims of education—its influence on character as well as on knowledge.

Measuring the enduring effects of education had long been beyond the reach of conventional research. The vast body of educational testing and research, despite its great scale and variety, dealt almost exclusively with young children or youth measured at one or more points during school or college or at the point of departure, and therefore at best answered only the question of the *immediate* effects of education. When individuals are no longer captives of the educational institution but have moved out into the wide adult world, they become fugitives. An investigator following a conventional research strategy must wait for years while the former students mature and age to the point appropriate for assessing enduring effects, then must track them down through a series of moves, often from old and out-of-date addresses, and try to persuade them to cooperate so as to measure the effects of earlier education. Such a strategy requires endless time and patience and much money, labor, and skill, all to be invested in a risky enterprise that may ultimately tap only a small and biased sample of the original population. No wonder there has been so little evidence on enduring effects of education.

Feldman and Newcomb summarized the state of such research in 1969, after completing an encyclopedic review of 1,500 studies conducted over a forty-year period in *The Impact of College on Students*: "College is supposed to do something to students, and that something refers primarily to consequences that make a difference in later years. There is, therefore, a very special irony in the fact that few studies of post-college persistence of such effects, especially those justifying confident conclusions, have been reported."

The few studies they cite illustrate vividly the limitations of that body of research. Bender followed up 112 Dartmouth students whose values had been studied during college, located 84 of them, and measured persistence and change up to about age thirty-five; Nelson followed up students from church-related colleges, located about 20% of the original group at about age thirty-five, and examined their religious values; Freedman et al. examined value changes in about 500 Vassar College alumnae; Newcomb's classic and almost unique study examined value changes in about 300 Bennington College alumnae when they had reached about age forty-five.[2]

Given the obstacles to conventional studies, the state of such research can have improved very little since 1969, and studies of enduring effects of *high-school* education, not within the scope of the Feldman-Newcomb review but surely as important, are equally scarce, since they are afflicted by the same difficulties. Our own review of that recent literature, not encyclopedic but far from cursory, documented new and important contributions to the study of the *immediate* and short-term effects but again revealed the void in the study of long-term *noneconomic* effects.[3]

A Design for Studying Lasting Effects

The unconventional strategy that has guided our research involves the "secondary analysis" of available sample surveys. With this strategy, adults are no longer fugitives who must be tracked down. Hundreds of thousands have already been captured by hundreds of national surveys that major agencies have routinely conducted over the past twenty-five years, using good sampling methods. Their ages, educational attainments, knowledge, and values have already been measured and filed in special archives waiting for secondary analysts to exploit such data for purposes other than those that inspired the original surveys. The surveys also measured other characteristics—sex, religion, race, ethnicity, and social, regional, and residential background—that might have influenced both educational attainment and the subjects' knowledge and values, and these had to be controlled to prevent spurious conclusions about the effects of education. Many conceive of the surveys simply as samplings of the "citizenry" or the "public." It requires only a shift in perspective to see that they are also samples of the *alumni* of all the nation's schools and colleges who, depending on their ages at the times of the surveys, represent specific classes. For example, the high-school and college graduates of the 1920s arrived at some specified life stage at a certain distance from their education—for example, "middle age" at the time of a 1950 survey or "old age" at the time of a 1970 survey. So long as they are still alive and at large within the continental boundaries of the United States, they are bound to be caught in the net of good national samplings, then classified and measured in the course of inquiry. Many conceive of these surveys simply as opinion polls. It requires only another shift in perspective to notice that the surveys often test knowledge and measure values. Seen in this unusual light, the surveys provided the raw materials from which we designed and fashioned both our earlier and our current studies of the enduring effects of education. Since the basic designs of the two studies are the same, readers familiar with our earlier work can skim the rest of this section and move quickly on to the detailed review of the selection and measurement of values that follows.

Thirty-eight national surveys containing the measures of values soon to be described, each designed to approach the ideal of an unbiased sample of the noninstitutionalized adult population, provide the data for the current study. As in the first study, no surveys before 1949 were included because the sampling up to then was sometimes not so well designed or executed. From the relevant later surveys we chose those that spanned the 1950s and 1960s and tried to cluster them around four points in time so as to assess educational effects as the schools went through several cycles of operation and as their students functioned in several historical contexts. The findings from both our studies are keyed to the same long period and to shorter phases within it, and thus we can compare the effects of the same educational experiences on cognition and on values. However, since some time had passed since we acquired and analyzed the data for our first study, we were able to extend the span of the current study to include a cluster of surveys conducted between 1970 and 1975, thus increasing the generalizability of the findings on values.[4] As in the first study, we chose all the surveys and the items within them "blindly," before inspecting any tables on the relation between education and values, so as to avoid any insidious tendency to invent some apparently plausible reason to exclude surveys or variables that yielded data against a hypothesis we might have favored.[5]

Inevitably, all sampling of human populations departs in practice from the ideal. Some misfortune may fall upon the best-designed survey, some error may creep in, and by chance alone an unbiased and well-executed sample may be just that one in a hundred that produces a result far from the truth. Our overall conclusions, however, are based on thirty-eight national surveys —one bad sample is only a drop in the large pool of data. The conclusions for the 1950s are based on fourteen surveys, those for the 1960s on fifteen surveys, and those for the early 1970s on nine surveys. One line of protection against error—there are others to be mentioned—is the large number of surveys included.

Some may entertain the idea that the routine practices of a particular survey agency may produce a systematic error or bias in all its surveys. Against this danger there is no safeguard in sheer number of surveys. Our surveys are the work of two agencies: twenty-six were conducted by the Gallup Organization and twelve by the National Opinion Research Center (NORC). Since the NORC material tended to be much richer in the number of measures of values, it turned out that almost exactly half (54%) of the tests of the enduring effects of education on values are from the NORC surveys. Thus any chronic bias in the sampling, and in the interviewing and measurement process as well, of either agency is counterbalanced by the equal weight of the data from the other agency. Tier A of table B.1 in Appendix B presents in greater detail the distribution of the thirty-eight surveys through the period 1949 to 1975.

In our first study, we presented evidence for a number of the surveys from the 1960s to show that the various educational levels of the population have been sampled and measured with high accuracy. Let us stress again that the apparent sampling bias in the earlier surveys—some tendency to overrepresent the better-educated groups in the population—cannot distort our conclusions about the general effects of education, or the differential effects in contrasted historical periods, derived from one of our two major modes of analysis. Since the sample is divided into separate educational groups that are then compared in values and knowledge, it does not matter if we have too few of one group and too many of another. Any improper weight in the aggregate makes no difference in such comparisons.[6] By contrast, summary statistical measures of the association between education and values over the *whole* sample could be influenced by any improper weights in the educational strata, and a bit more caution should be applied to these findings.

Four age-groups or life stages have been separately examined in each of the surveys. Individuals under age twenty-five were eliminated from all analyses, thereby insuring that almost all the adults studied had completed their formal education.[7] It would hardly be fair to include among "enduring" effects those that stem from continuing exposure to school. Equally important, this exclusion protects us against a sampling bias that may affect all the surveys because the agencies must limit themselves to sampling the noninstitutionalized population. Since a fairly large and perhaps distinctive segment of the adults in their early twenties may be members of the military or attending residential colleges, generalizations about the effects of education on all young adults based on samples of those outside institutions could be in error.

In the current study, with some minor exceptions to be noted, we have once again eliminated individuals over age seventy-two. Since a considerable portion of the very old are in institutions, one should not generalize about all the oldest adults through the sampling designs employed in these surveys. Also, some unknown portion of the oldest adults who are living in private households and thus are reached by the samplings may excuse themselves or have to be eliminated at the point of inquiry because of illness, deafness, blindness, or infirmity; or, if interviewed, they may not function at their best. Some may argue that those who have survived to very advanced ages, no matter what their condition, especially those who have remained well enough to be home and be interviewed, are a peculiar, hardy breed. Eliminating the very old from the analyses thus protects our conclusions against such sources of error, though it limits generalizations to effects that have endured up to but not beyond age seventy-two.

By now the reader can see how the studies of enduring effects on cognition and on values have been meshed into the same cycles of the educational system and the same historical contexts, and also keyed to the same birth cohorts of specific social composition examined at the same life stages. Thus we shall be able to draw a *profile* of effects and establish whether education has produced both a growth of knowledge and an enrichment of values or whether the effects in the realm of values fail to match the large effects we have found on cognition. And by tracing these effects through successively advanced life stages, we can establish how long the two classes of effects endure.

Within any single survey or set of surveys clustered around the same point in time—for example, 1970—comparing the relative effects of education across the four age-groups may at first seem to be truly a moving picture of the wearing away, persistence, or consolidation of the effects of education with aging. Although the groups have reached successively advanced stages of life, we must realize that the same birth cohort cannot be tracked by a single survey as it moves on through life. The youngest adults in 1970 are the products of the colleges of the 1960s and represent the World War II generation, whereas the oldest adults represent the World War I generation or earlier and the colleges of the 1930s or before. Thus there is some obscurity in any single set of such comparisons. But if we find a uniform pattern in such comparisons from several sets of surveys from different time periods, no matter what birth cohorts and historical experiences were involved, it seems safe to generalize about the effects that emerge with aging.

We have, however, employed another mode of analysis to eliminate the obscurity in this picture. The very same birth cohort studied in an early survey can be traced and located again in a later survey, after it has aged some specified number of years. For example, the cohort that was twenty-five to thirty-six in a 1951 survey has become the age-group thirty-seven to forty-eight in a 1963 survey; those who were thirty-seven to forty-eight in the 1951 survey have become forty-nine to sixty by 1963. Although our surveys do not include a panel or a longitudinal study of the very same individuals, they yield something almost as good: equivalent national samples of a given birth cohort and the educational strata within it studied at several points along the life course. As a group moves further and further away from its earlier exposure to education, the pattern can be described—for more than one birth cohort and for various phases of the aging process—simply by juxtaposing the appropriate groups in the different surveys. For example, a number of cohorts were reexamined after twenty years had passed, when the members of one cohort had reached old age.

By the time any cohort reaches a very advanced age, it has experienced much attrition, and the survivors still at large are the only members who remain to be sampled. To reduce error in generalizing about aging and its effects on the basis of the very select group that may have survived, we have not pushed these analyses beyond the point where individuals have reached their early seventies.[11] But we have controlled such error in other ways. Because whites in America have had a better chance to survive, in any such analysis based on *unrestricted* samples the findings might reflect the different racial composition of the contrasted age levels rather than the sheer fact of aging. But since all the comparisons are restricted to whites, the danger of a false conclusion is automatically avoided. This was one more benefit from the decision to exclude blacks from the study.[12]

The accuracy of the findings from these cohort analyses also depends on the equivalence of the instruments used in the various surveys. Otherwise the changes observed might reflect changes in the instruments as well as changes arising from sheer aging. Many of the questions on values, repeatedly employed by the agencies over a long period to describe long-term trends, were ideally suited for the cohort analyses and also for comparing the effects of education in different periods, where equivalence of instruments is also a requirement.[13] The availability of identical questions was one major reason for including particular sets of surveys and particular values in the study. This brings us to the choice of the values used to assess the effects of education and how they were measured.

The Selection and Measurement of Values

The fifty-five surveys included in our earlier study contained 250 questions that measured a wide variety of discrete bits of knowledge in a number of different domains. Many of the items tested "academic" knowledge of facts in geography, history, science, and humanities that were or might have been taught during the adult's earlier schooling. Other items tested knowledge of current affairs and contemporary public figures in domestic and foreign politics and in popular culture. These items indirectly tested receptivity to new knowledge, since adults could obtain such knowledge only by making use of current sources of information. Fifty more questions directly asked about information-seeking: about deliberate exposure to mass media, interpersonal sources of information, and adult education. We found almost without exception that all the discrete bits and all the kinds of knowledge gleaned, as well as the seeking after knowledge, were substantially increased by education.

Some may argue about the precise weight a discrete finding should have been given in our earlier overall conclusions, since some bits of knowledge that were measured were trivial in contrast with other more important bits. Whatever the precise weights, however, one cannot reject the assumption that gains in *every kind* of knowledge, no matter how trivial, should have been credited to education. Surely it is not *bad* to be informed about anything or to be trying to learn about it. Thus the inclusion of items was no problem in the earlier study. All the available questions in the period spanned were relevant, deserved to be included, and created no perplexity in drawing conclusions. By contrast, selecting items as criteria of the effects of education in the current study presented real problems, since there could be serious disagreement on whether some values are "good" or "bad." Indeed, we found considerable disagreement between ourselves over some of the questions considered, and even where we agreed we realized that others would not always share our judgment on the goodness of the value being measured. If we included too many such items among the criterion measures, no matter how accurate and generalizable the findings, the final conclusions would be debatable. There is no way to eliminate all such controversy, but we have tried to reduce it by studying a limited realm of values that most reasonable judges would agree are "good" or "bad," still leaving the areas tapped broad enough to permit general conclusions about the effects of education on a variety of important values.[14]

Given the usual definition of a value, it might also have seemed sensible to use questions that elicited the respondent's generalized expression of his desire for certain end-states and patterns of conduct and social relations, or his opinion on their general desirability, these values being ones whose moral worth or goodness most reasonable judges would agree upon.[15] Who could argue the case against peace, harmony, freedom or liberty, equality, nonviolence, honesty, truth, beauty, love? If such values were then found to be more prevalent, or less prevalent, in the better-educated stratum in our national samples, that would seem to provide the most unassailable evidence.

It might seem to be our sad fate as secondary analysts that the surveys hardly ever ask such general questions. In fact it may be our salvation. The values that most reasonable judges could agree upon would also be endorsed by most reasonable respondents in our samples. Practically everyone favors them. The skeptic about survey research also could argue that normal respondents know they *ought* to hold such values and often will *say* they do even if deep down in their hearts they cherish opposing or evil values. The survey agencies, knowing that such values prevail, and that direct general questions are insensitive and perhaps subject to response bias, therefore rarely formulate questions in such terms.[16]

Very occasionally in the recent period, survey researchers have studied values with a complex instrument that does not suffer from the deficiencies just noted. A long list of general values (as many as 18) is presented, and the respondent ranks them from first to last or arranges them in a cruder order, for example, top and bottom three, by relative importance. Since all the values presented are worthy, the instrument is not susceptible to response bias. No matter which values the respondent ranks high, he cannot present himself in an unattractive light. By measuring the hierarchy of values, just how important a value is compared with others, the instrument relates trenchantly to the conflictful situations of real life, where one value may have to be sacrificed to an overriding value.[17]

Two of our surveys in the 1970s contained such an instrument. Those data have been included in our analysis and will be presented below, but none of our other surveys measured general values directly, for the obvious reasons noted earlier and for other good reasons as well. Just as we all have observed in real life the paradox that men who value peace sometimes are in favor of war, the survey agencies again and again have observed that respondents who endorsed a *general* value will then take a contradictory position on a subsequent question involving a specific application of that value. To cite one such illustration, surveys have found among those who valued freedom of speech in general that a large percentage opposed the freedom of American socialists to publish newspapers and of American communists to speak on radio.[18] Such contradictions do not mean that the respondents are flagrant liars or simply giving lip service to a value, but rather demonstrate that many people do not see that a general value they hold is implicated at all in specific situations. They do not make the connection. The value is not *engaged*, not aroused in the mind, by the circumstances described and thus is not applied to the concrete case. Or people may see some special ground for removing the case from the jurisdiction of the value—for example, defining socialists or communists as some special breed not entitled to the same freedom as others. Or the specific situation may arouse conflicting values, such as freedom and national security, the former being sacrificed to the latter in the instance mentioned.

For such reasons, the survey agencies usually ask questions that involve the application of one or more values to a specific situation or that follow an initial general value question with a string of subquestions describing specific situations. Perforce, we must use such specific questions as criteria of the effects of education, but we do so willingly, since they provide sharper, more accurate, and more demanding tests.[19] Admittedly, by its very specificity each such test explores only one or a few of the many situations where the value might apply. But since batteries of questions were available for most of the values, the combined or cumulative evidence from the various tests establishes whether individuals and groups show enough consistency to justify the assertion that they hold a particular general value.

Such instruments seem to us highly appropriate to the problem under study. If education is to be effective, it cannot merely inculcate values in the abstract. Those values might then remain inert. It must make an individual more alert and sensitive to the situations where particular values are implicated so that they more readily become engaged and must also help him weigh the conflicting claims of several values that he has become sensitive enough to see as relevant to a complex situation. To be sure, some of the questions employed may create a new source of controversy about our conclusions, even when there is agreement on the goodness of a particular value. Some judges might disagree with our judgment that a particular good value should take precedence over another value that is also implicated in the complex situation described in a question, or they might even deny its relevance. But not many such dubious or ambiguous questions can have survived the protracted debate between us, and those that remain carry little weight in the overall findings from the many tests. We shall alert the reader to these occasional controversial items so that he can weigh them for himself, although it is highly unlikely that the general conclusions will be affected.

Many of the national surveys open one other avenue to the study of values. Questions about desirable forms of conduct such as voting in elections, contributing to political parties, and writing letters to public officials have been asked frequently over the years. By any definition, actions are not values, but since they are guided or inspired to some degree by values, it may seem strange that we have used no such questions on conduct. To some extent these tests have already been made. In one of the few secondary analyses of the enduring effects of college education, Withey demonstrated over a series of surveys that such political actions are much more characteristic of college-educated adults than of those who have not gone to college, and he and others have shown that such differences cannot be explained away by errors or biases in the measurement of such acts.[20] However, these kinds of data could have been subjected to deeper analysis in the course of our study. Withey and his colleagues were not concerned with how long the effects endured over the course of aging and therefore did no cohort analyses. Distinctions between those with high-school and grade-school educations were not introduced, since the authors were exclusively interested in the effect of college, and the influence of intermediate education on such conduct thus remains to be determined. It may seem strange that we did not follow the path they marked out and exploit these possible criterion measures. However appealing the path may be to some, it is a treacherous one and may not lead to safe conclusions about effects on values. Consider one example cited above. That the less educated are less likely to make political contributions may not mean they have less civic virtue or that they do not value political involvement. It may simply mean that they have less money at their disposal, since education is highly correlated with economic advantage. In the same vein, that an uneducated man makes few or no contributions to charity should not be taken to mean that he does not value charity and helpfulness to others. However generous he might wish to be, he may be too poor to engage in philanthropy.

To formulate it generally, comparisons of conduct do not provide fair tests of differences in values, for in such contests over virtue the uneducated are handicapped by the constraints upon them and the educated are advantaged by their opportunities. At a subtler level, such a handicap can account for the dramatic fact that the college-educated are more than twice as likely to have written to a public official. Writing—one of the three Rs—is a skill that grows with education, and the parsimonious explanation of the finding is that the uneducated endorse the value but lack the skill. Other factors also obscure the meaning of conduct questions as measures of values. The much lower rate of voting among the lesser educated and uneducated that Withey found in surveys of eight elections may reflect not only their lesser opportunity to vote each half receiving a different form of the instrument in which the wording or position of a question and the surrounding questions was varied, and in other surveys both halves receiving the same instrument, constituting a pure replication of the measurements and a test of random errors.

All these kinds of safeguards, and others to be described later, were built into our design in greater or lesser degree in the measurement of each of the values in the different time periods. In presenting the findings, we average the results from the many discrete tests to yield a summary measure that attenuates the errors peculiar to given questions, an entire survey, or the work of one agency, and that also compresses the many findings into a simple, comprehensible form that is indicative of the general value that prevails across diverse situations. But the results for each of the 151 discrete tests are also presented separately—partly to show whether subjects apply the values in a discriminating way dependent on the concrete situations described in the questions and partly as empirical evidence of how susceptible the measurements are to errors. Contrary to what some might expect, the values for the various educational groups are highly stable no matter what the procedure, thus suggesting that random error and biasing errors characterizing particular agencies are small in magnitude.

The skeptic, however, might still not be convinced of the accuracy of measurement, seeing the specter of a "social desirability" bias that afflicts *all* the measurements of values, regardless of agency, survey, or question. Presumably under every condition the respondents are motivated to deny that they hold "bad" values and to make false claims about their "good" values to gain approval. That could be considered a problem had we used the data from direct general questions on whether the respondents favored equality, honesty, freedom, and so on, or had engaged in virtuous conduct. But even then serious worries might not be warranted. If respondents are so strongly motivated to exaggerate their virtue, is it not strange that in survey after survey fewer than 6% claim to have worked in a political campaign and only 10% to 20% claim to have ever written a letter to a public official? Is it not surprising that those who falsely claimed they had voted in the 1964 election (as determined from voting records) constituted less than 8% of the national sample, and that a similar check in the classic survey in Elmira during the 1948 election found that 98% of the sample were truthful about their voting?[25] Adults apparently have no strong and pervasive need to exaggerate their virtues when talking anonymously to skilled, strange interviewers during well-conducted surveys; or else it is much less obvious to the subjects themselves wherein virtue lies and how best to simulate it than it is to the skeptic.[26]

Whatever worries a skeptic might still entertain about how vulnerable *general* questions are to social desirability bias surely do not apply to the highly specific questions we have employed as measures of values. Appendix A lists all the questions we have used, with their exact wording and any original prefatory statements used. Since most of the questions were used repeatedly in surveys over the years so that the agencies could measure long-term trends, we could thus assess the relative effects of education in different historical periods by identical measures. Correspondingly, the agencies would have accumulated a great deal of information from the interviewers and from analysis of the questions' susceptibility to various kinds of errors and biases, and they no doubt would have changed the wording or scrapped entire questions if experience had shown them unsatisfactory. To be sure, the agencies are not infallible, and an occasional blemished question might have been retained to keep monitoring an important social trend. But it is highly unlikely that many seriously deficient questions could have stood the test of time and remained in the pool of items the agencies continued to use.[27] We ourselves have carefully scrutinized all those items that were left in the pool, in light of our own long experience in survey research, and we scrapped some despite their relevance because we feared they might yield dubious measures of the particular values.

Reading Appendix A will show that on many questions it is not easy for a respondent to decide which answer is appropriate if he wishes to show himself in a desirable light. Consider the battery of trend questions used to measure the value of civil liberties for nonconformists. If the respondent answers some questions so as to enhance his image as a libertarian, he runs the risk of showing himself in sympathy with communists and atheists, which are anathema to many people. If he portrays himself as untainted by such sympathies, he shows illiberalism. On other questions, if he presents himself in a desirable light as a supporter of academic freedom, he runs the risk of seeming unconcerned about protecting impressionable youth from subversive teachers—surely not an attractive way to present oneself. In many of our questions, the quantum of social desirability bias is divided, and neither of the major alternative answers a respondent might give is handicapped or advantaged.[28]

Careful reading of the questions will reveal other subtle features that protect the inference from biasing errors. Note the preface to the battery of questions on liberty for nonconformists. Since it is not contained within the "question" it might be missed in a hasty reading, but it is an integral part of the measuring instrument. It tells the respondent that "there are always some people whose ideas are considered bad or dangerous by other people," thus suggesting that if he wishes to present himself in a "favorable" light, he should opt to hamper the liberties of "bad or dangerous" nonconformists. We, like Stouffer, score the endorsement of liberty as a "good" value, and that value is not inflated by social desirability bias, since the introduction has deliberately added the extra weight of such a bias to the *alternative* answer.

Some of the questions, it can be noted, are identical except that a prefatory statement of the kind just reviewed may be added or omitted in one survey or another. Social desirability bias is therefore not equally present in both instances, and comparing the two findings in fact constitutes an experimental test of the influence of social desirability on respondents and their answers. The profiles of the various educational groups tend to be stable despite the manipulation, suggesting that the bias—whatever its force—is constant in magnitude for all the groups. So long as the bias is a constant, it cannot distort the comparisons by educational level.

Skimming over other questions listed in Appendix A, one can see that social desirability bias often would not operate in *one* direction to distort the *national* survey findings. For example, in the battery on abortion, one question deals with the mother's right to obtain a legal abortion when the child may be born deformed. We scored endorsement of this as indicative of a humane and "good" value. Perhaps an atheist might endorse that right so as to appear more socially desirable, but an orthodox Catholic probably would not assume that posture to gain approval in his own circles.[29] Some questions that are used as measures of the good value *equality* are couched in terms of support for the equal rights of blacks. A Southerner seeking to appear more socially desirable in the era when some of the surveys were conducted would not have been likely to endorse that value, though a Northerner might have gained in prestige by doing so. On our questions, the force of social desirability bias is bound to be fragmented within any nationwide educational category because of its heterogeneity and the differing conceptions of the desirable in its component groupings. The *net* effect of such a bias might be so small that it would have very little effect on the comparisons between educational levels. Yet the contrasted educational levels, all of them heterogenerous categories nationwide, do differ in social composition. Therefore the net effect, however small, might not be constant in direction and magnitude and might distort the comparisons. However, when we control religion, region, and so forth, and compare educational levels that are then equivalent in social composition, as we shall be doing for reasons to be described, any social desirability bias tends to become constant in magnitude and direction.

The skeptic, despite all this logic and evidence to the contrary, might argue on one last ground that social desirability bias would be more likely to influence the answers of the better-educated, thus exaggerating conclusions about the good effects of education. Even if everyone felt equally concerned to present himself in an attractive way, the greater sensitivity of the educated to the nuances of language and any tendencies toward more polite forms of expression could cause more social desirability bias in their answers to certain questions. Stember was alert to this danger when in the course of an early, almost unique, example of a secondary analysis of the effects of education he obtained highly generalizable evidence that education reduced some, but not all, forms of prejudice. He warns us that "the educated . . . probably recognize and avoid the trap set by a crudely phrased question. While rejecting, as they often do, a stereotype phrased in obviously biased cliches, they may nevertheless agree with its substance. . . . Various subcultural segments of the

16

population have their own modes of speech, some characteristically vehement or uninhibited, others more restrained. The educated tend to shun the vocabulary of the blatant bigot."[30] Thus he discounted the finding that education reduces endorsement of the stereotype "Jewish businessmen . . . are so shrewd and tricky that other people do not have a fair chance in competition," since the educated endorse the parallel statement that Jews "are not as good as other people in being fair in business," revealing prejudice similar in substance to that of the uneducated when "intemperate, hostile language" is eliminated from the question.[31] Stember therefore relied on many different kinds of questions from many national surveys in the years 1944–59 to arrive at conclusions that are generalizable and not vulnerable to such biases in measurement.

We too rely on many different kinds of questions. Very few involve simple traps that would catch only the verbally unsophisticated or are couched in crude language that might be acceptable only to the uneducated and thus might handicap them in comparisons with the educated. Some questions do contain emotionally laden terms, presumably more appealing to the lesser educated and leading them to respond to the symbol rather than the substance of the issue. Let us stress, however, that, in real life, value questions are often inextricably bound up with emotion and often formulated in emotionally loaded terms by parties in conflict over the issue. The emotional tone is not something arbitrarily added to some of our questions by the pollster, but makes them a more faithful presentation of reality and better predictors of whether the value would be applied by the respective educational groups. Let us also stress that the emotional terms in such questions may push the respondent in the direction of a "good" or socially desirable answer as often as they push him toward endorsing the "bad" or socially undesirable answer. If there is a greater tendency for the uneducated to respond to loaded symbols, it could *advantage* them in comparisons with the educated about as often as it handicaps them. The exact wordings of all the questions are open to scrutiny. Special semantic features that might affect findings from specific questions will be noted. And comparing the findings from such questions with results from questions similar in substance but different in form provides a test of this possible source of social desirability bias that will allay skepticism.

For all the reasons reviewed, the *general* conclusions about the effects of education are well protected against errors related to social desirability bias. But in drawing conclusions about the *relative* effects of education in different historical periods, social desirability bias might create a problem. In the twenty-five years spanned by our surveys, there have been widespread, dramatic changes in some values. For example, during the time of the Cold War and McCarthyism, there was a steady decline in support for civil liberties for nonconformists. That trend was then reversed, and the value has revived and gained many supporters in recent years.[32] By contrast, the value of equality as applied to racial groups has grown steadily throughout the entire long span under study.[33] Indeed, the gradual growth of support for those values in the national population in itself is indirect but powerful evidence of the good effects of education. It can be accounted for, in part, simply by the expansion of educational opportunity in America. As the cohorts born long ago and therefore less educationally advantaged have died off and been replaced by newer, more educated cohorts, some shift in the nation's values has come about just because of the increasing weight of more educated people in the population, who were also found to be more equalitarian and libertarian.[34]

Although these long-term nationwide trends are welcome evidence of the good effects of education, they may create a problem in accurately assessing the *relative* effects of the education provided in different periods. A national trend that reaches landslide proportions might turn social desirability bias from a fragmented and trivial force in an earlier period into a more unidirectional and stronger force in a later period. Individuals who do not share the pervasive value, *if they sense* that they are unfashionable, out of tune with the times, might feel considerable pressure to falsify their answers. There is, however, a built-in safeguard that operates in such times to counterbalance the increased risk of bias. In the very nature of the process, the greater the numbers whose pressure might be felt, the smaller the minority who are under pressure to make false reports. The magnitude of the error is bound to become less and less as the risk of bias increases. And since not all members of the minority *perceive* that they are, in fact, out of tune with the times, some would feel no pressure at all to falsify their values. Thus the magnitude of the error is reduced even further.[35] At worst, the comparisons of educational groups would be distorted very little by the residual error. Since it is reasonable to assume that the small error affects all the educational groups equally,[36] it is likely that it does not distort the comparisons at all. Even in such a period, the *difference* in the values of the educational groups would still be accurately revealed.

No matter what the nature of the times when particular surveys were conducted, social desirability bias cannot distort the comparisons of educational groups. However, the real and widespread growth of a "good" value in a particular period, plus whatever small bias accompanies and exaggerates such a national trend, does make it more difficult to demonstrate any gain that might have been produced by more education and to assess the *relative* effects of the education provided in different historical periods. Since each question provides only a limited number of alternative answers, when the point is reached on any question that very large numbers give the only answer indicative of the "good" value, there is little room left for the educated to reveal any superior values they might hold. Although identical questions or measuring instruments are used across the different periods, the population may score closer to the 'ceiling" of an instrument in one period and closer to the "floor" in another period, and the relative effects of education may appear smaller in the first instance and larger in the second. The problem is solved, as in our first study, by computing indexes of "effectiveness" whenever necessary, which take account of the distance to the ceiling of the instrument by expressing the absolute differences between educational groups as a ratio of the maximum gain possible in that period. The computation of the index, its properties, various uses,[37] and interpretation will be reviewed later when we present specific findings based on its application.

Establishing the Effects of Education

The gross differences in the prevalence of "good" values in groups contrasted in levels of educational attainment, however accurately and comprehensively measured, cannot be accepted immediately and uncritically as proof of the effects of education. As in our earlier study of cognitive effects, there is danger that hasty conclusions about effects on values might be spurious. At times during the long period—almost a century—brought under scrutiny by the time span of our surveys and by the wide age range of the respondents included, opportunity to start and to complete a long course of education has been far from equal. The various factors that governed selective educational attainment might also have determined the values. The groups who ended up with more education might well have differed *initially* in values or have arrived at their ultimately different values for reasons having nothing to do with their education. For example, whites growing up in the North have tended to get more education than whites in the South, and any greater support of racial equality observed among the educated might simply reflect the disproportionate number of northerners in that cell and the effects of the northern milieu rather than the effects of formal education. To take a more paradoxical example, blacks have suffered severe educational handicaps in contrast with whites. In a gross comparison, if the *lesser* educated were found to be more supportive of the value of racial equality than the more educated, it could not be taken to mean that education has a deleterious effect. Since the racial composition of the two groups has not been equated, it is not a fair test. Even if better-educated whites were more egalitarian than less-educated whites, that fact could have been obscured in a gross comparison by the overlay and disproportionate number of blacks in the uneducated cell.

Conclusions about the effects of education on values must be protected by adequate controls over the major factors that have accounted for selective educational attainment at any point during the long period under study and that also might affect the values implicated in the specific questions we have examined.

Two of these factors, as in our earlier study, have been routinely controlled throughout all the tests of the effects of education on values. Age may influence values because of the changing ethos of the historical periods in which earlier and later generations were born and socialized (apart from the change in perspectives created just by growing older), and it also has been a major determinant of educational attainment, because of the gradual and continuous

19

expansion of educational opportunity. Thus in any gross comparison of more- and less-educated respondents one is comparing younger individuals with older individuals, recent generations with earlier generations. However, age is controlled, as noted earlier, because all the comparisons of educational levels are age-specific, each involving only individuals within a narrow age-band and representing a specific, relatively homogeneous group or generation born in a particular historical period. Similarly, to reduce errors in sampling and measurement and various ambiguities that might otherwise complicate inferences about changes as a cohort ages, the black respondents were excluded from all the surveys from the beginning, and all comparisons and findings were restricted to the white population. Thus race was automatically controlled, eliminating another major source of spuriousness. Blacks, of course, have had far less opportunity for education than whites and might well differ in values for many reasons stemming from circumstances other than education.

Six other social factors that have been found to affect educational attainment at some time during the long period under study and that might influence the particular values we have examined have also been controlled.[38] Sex, recorded in all the surveys, was controlled in all tests. Religion, ethnicity (American vs. foreign birthplace), social-class origins, and residential origins (size of community and region where the respondent was born) were controlled in many, though not all, of the tests, since not all of these variables were included in every survey from which our questions were drawn. The control on ethnicity insures that we are examining the effects of *American* education, since some of the foreign-born might reflect the influences of the education they had received elsewhere before immigrating into the United States. And the many other controls not only safeguard the general conclusions but also permit us to examine whether education has differential effects on values in particular social groups. Such a hypothesis seems plausible, since some groups might initially be more resistant to the value changes education might initiate, and in later life might be placed in milieus that are more or less conducive to maintaining the values education taught them. For example, southerners and northerners might differ in the strength of their initial position on racial equality, and the forces brought to bear upon them in later life would be more or less powerful in assailing the value of equality.

These eight factors, of course, do not exhaust the determinants of a person's values. Considerable variance in values or in specific attitudes that implicate values remains unexplained in studies that measure and employ such social factors in quantitative analyses and predictions. Clinical and case studies reveal idiosyncratic experiences that shape the values of particular individuals—an accident, a chance encounter, a trauma, a particularly potent teacher or preacher or neighbor, even a distant or historical figure taken as a model or reference individual. Such variables cannot be controlled, since some are beyond anyone's current knowledge and others cannot be known without deep inquiry. But there is every reason to assume that the distribution of such idiosyncratic factors, such accidental experiences, is helter-skelter, falling here and there at random rather than piling up in any particular location. Such factors therefore need not be controlled. Unless they are related to *educational attainment*, they cannot account for the influence of education on values, since they would be equally present or absent in all the educational groups compared.

The eight variables directly controlled in our comparisons of educational attainment have been found to be major social factors influencing educational attainment, but of course there are other factors influencing educational attainment that we have not been able to control directly. But unless such other factors also have an independent influence on *values*, they cannot possibly account for or explain away any effects education has on values and need not be controlled in the comparisons. And an invisible but powerful set of controls over *all* the social sources of selective educational attainment has been introduced indirectly by the design of our study. Over the long period spanned by our surveys and the birth cohorts within them, there has been a great expansion of educational opportunity. In the population from which our oldest cohort was drawn—those over sixty in the surveys conducted about 1950, some of whom were born as early as 1877—only about 8% had gone to college and only about 20% had been fortunate enough to have *any* high-school training. Those born twenty years later, but still around the turn of the century, had double the opportunities. About 15% had gone to college and about one-third had some high school. For the youngest adults in our surveys about 1970—those born about 1940—educational opportunity had so expanded that almost one-third had gone to college and almost two-thirds had gone to high school. Over the many cohorts, the implicit contrast is between education conferred on a small, highly selected social elite and education provided for a relatively unselected mass.[39] If selectivity accounted for our findings, the gross effects of education should be reduced in our more recent surveys and cohorts, where control of selective social factors, though not complete, has automatically become stronger and stronger.

Despite all the controls, direct and indirect, a critic may still argue that some factor remains uncontrolled that accounts both for greater educational attainment and values. But it would be unreasonable for him to demand that the contrasted educational groups be equated in every respect as they would be if a perfect experiment had been conducted on a grand scale—as if groups had been assigned at random to receive more or less education and forced to complete whatever amount of education had been allocated to them. No such experiment has ever been conducted, and probably none ever will be. If our findings on the effects of education are spurious, they should be radically reduced by controlling so many of the factors that have been found to be important determinants of educational attainment. Whatever factors remain uncontrolled should not be taken seriously unless one can document their substantial influence on educational attainment *after* our controls have been

21

applied and also make a good argument, on an empirical or theoretical basis, that they would influence the values examined. Some of the differences between educational groups that might persist despite our controls can be discounted as determinants of values.[40] Other variables must be given more careful consideration.

Since it is impossible to measure the intelligence and propensity toward learning that an individual had in *early childhood* before being educated, there can be no direct control over these factors in surveys of adults. Consequently, in our first study, which focused on the enduring effects of education on knowledge, receptivity to knowledge, and active information-seeking, much attention had to be given to this source of spurious conclusions. The better-educated adults might have been admitted to and completed their longer course of education because of their initially greater intellectual abilities and propensities and might have become more knowledgeable in later life simply through exercising those talents and drives rather than as a result of their education. However, because of the substantial correlation between class and intelligence, the controls on social origins employed in both our studies eliminate considerable variation in intelligence that would otherwise be present in comparisons of educational groups and therefore reduce the danger of spurious conclusions. Some residual variation in intelligence still remains after these indirect controls are imposed and may inflate the apparent effects of education. The degree to which this endangered the conclusions of the first study was carefully appraised in light of the literature on the relation between intelligence and educational attainment and turned out to be far less than we feared. The correlations vary from study to study depending on the population, period, and procedures; the variance in education explained by intelligence often is surprisingly low and depends on what level of education—for example, high school vs. college entrance vs. college graduation—is being examined; often is an *inflated* estimate because intelligence frequently is measured after some schooling and thus reflects in part the effect of education.[41]

The fact that the influence of intelligence has changed over time and has been found to be differentially important for the educational attainment of various groups—for example, boys vs. girls, lower vs. upper classes—provided an analytical tool for appraising whether it accounted for our earlier findings. If it did, the effects of education should have been more marked in particular subgroups and time periods. The review of these findings and indirect avenues to solution of the problem is detailed and complex, and we shall not repeat it.[42] The clear conclusion is that even in the study of effects of education on *knowledge* the lack of direct control of ability and propensity creates little danger. The danger would be smaller yet in our current study. Intelligence and inclinations toward study obviously have relevance for the acquisition of *knowledge* and for the special value implicated in the process of learning—a love of knowledge or truth. But for the range of values we have studied, freedom, liberty, equality, and the like, it is equally obvious that these factors are far less important. If sheer ability and studiousness determined such values, virtue and goodness would be far more prevalent in certain circles.

Despite the many direct controls on important determinants of values, a critic might note the inherent limitation of the design and argue that there is no measure of or direct control over initial differences in the values of the contrasted educational groups. But it would be arbitrary and unfounded to assert that, after taking account of religion and race, class, region, and so forth, there were substantial differences across the nation throughout this long period in the initial value profile of those who subsequently obtained more rather than less education. Surely the high schools, and probably most colleges, did not consciously select students on the basis of their initial values. Most of these institutions knew too little about the student's values or the determinants of such values to make their selections in such fashion. For every Reed College or Bennington that might have tried to handpick students or that would have attracted students with a particular profile of values, there would have been a Sweet Briar or a Virginia Military Institute that would have attracted or tried to handpick the opposite type.[43] Individuals entering different curricula and different colleges might differ in their initial values, but this does not imply that the aggregate of educated individuals across the nation would be homogeneous in their initial values and sharply different from the less-educated segments in the national population, taking account of other background characteristics.

Indeed, considerable empirical evidence suggests great initial heterogeneity in values among *college* entrants. If anything, the heterogeneity would be even greater in the far larger, less select nationwide group of those with high-school educations. In a paper aptly titled "The Myth of Unanimity," Peter Rose reported findings on the variability among freshmen entering the eleven colleges in the Connecticut Valley in 1963. On the endorsement of civil liberties for politically nonconformist students and professors—one of the very indicators of values we employ in our study—the percentage of freshmen supporting this value for professors ranged from 34% to 82%, and the support for nonconformist students ranged from 53% to 91%.[44] A fortiori, one would expect the variability to be even greater among freshmen in the hundreds of colleges across the nation. In their comprehensive review of studies of the influence of college, Feldman and Newcomb present many other compelling demonstrations of the great initial variability among freshmen even in a relatively *homogeneous* set of colleges. In one such study, for example, in 1959 Trent sampled freshmen in five West Coast Catholic colleges and administered a series of scales from the "Omnibus Personality Inventory." For first-year males in the five very similar schools, to cite only one finding, the mean score on "thinking introversion" (a liking for reflective thought rather than for practical matters) was 29, but the standard deviation was 9.3, showing a great deal of variability. Using the same instrument, the freshmen classes of eight rather varied colleges were studied by McConnell et al. The mean score for first-year males ranged from 16.03 at the University of Portland to 44.03 at Reed College. On a scale measuring authoritarianism, the mean score for first-year males ranged from 60.7 at the University of Portland, the most authoritarian group, to a mean of 101 for Reed first-year males, the least authoritarian group. Abe et al. surveyed freshmen at widely contrasted colleges in 1964. The percentage of first-year male students who stated that interracial dating was likely to lead to trouble ranged over three sharply contrasted schools from 30% to 62%; the percentage who stated that following a formal religious code was an essential life goal ranged from 7% to 43%.[45] The American Council on Education's continuing program of testing very large national samples of college freshmen provides additional evidence of the great *initial* variability in the population that has gone to college. Most of the measures, understandably, deal with variables relating to intellectual and academic matters, but some vividly demonstrate the variability in values. For example, among women students at four major types of colleges (public, private, religious, or secular in foundation), the percentages who attended Sunday school during their freshman year ranged from 19% to 45%; those who said grace before meals from 14% to 40%; those who prayed from 40% to 74%; those who attended church from 53% to 89%.[46] In light of such evidence, it is hardly tenable to think of each of our contrasted nationwide groups, high school as well as college, as being initially homogeneous in values and to discount enduring effects of education as being present before the experience.

The major factors *predating* education that might account both for selective attainment and for values have been brought under control and scrutiny. But endless experiences *postdating* education may have modified knowledge or values. As we stated in our earlier study:

> The influence of most of these variables need not be controlled. The unique feature of our study is the measurement of *enduring* effects of education. What one truly wants to know is whether the seeds of knowledge [or the values] ... will wither with time or endure throughout the vicissitudes of experience and into old age. The variables that time carries, however destructive their force or beneficent their influence, generally should not be controlled or eliminated in reckoning the effects of education, although it would be informative to unravel some of the complexities of the long process.
>
> In contrast, chains of *distinctive* experience that represent only the perpetuation (albeit in new forms) of the original advantages or handicaps that particular social groups had prior to their education should be controlled. But this has been accomplished automatically by the controls on the major social factors that determine selective educational attainment. Whatever later experiences are distinctive to whites, or women, or the offspring

of the poor, for example, have been equated when refined comparisons by education are made within groups homogeneous in such respects. . . .

In contrast with such distinctive experiences predetermined long ago, there are other, later chains of experience that begin to be forged simply as a result of education, whatever the person's initial status. These, too, need not be controlled. After all education can do its work only indirectly, once individuals have left school, through creating the links that join together a long causal process. . . .

An obvious link in the long chain of effect . . . is the life style that the educated can achieve. Educational credentials facilitate entry into privileged occupations. . . . Whether this link is essential to the process has been tested by introducing controls on current socioeconomic status. Such tests also incorporate and control whatever privileged position individuals may simply have "inherited" from their families.[47]

Other features of the contemporary milieu of the adults have also been controlled. For example, in examining the effects of education on the value of racial equality, we have controlled for residence in the South vs. other parts of the country. These and similar analyses to be presented later test whether the values inculcated by education can survive only when later life conditions are favorable to the maintenance of the value or whether they are retained under more stringent conditions, and thus will be dramatic evidence of the power of education as a force for good.

We have reviewed at some length the general problems that seem crucial in studying enduring effects of education: locating large and representative samples of adults of all ages who have been exposed to differing amounts of education in different historical periods; comprehensive and accurate measurement of values; coverage and accurate measurement of independent variables that might account for selective educational attainment and by themselves contribute to values so as to isolate the net effects of education; and tracing effects into old age to examine stability, growth, or decline with progressive aging. Other special problems that require consideration will be treated as we present the findings.

2 The Findings

The evidence on enduring effects of education is provided by 151 discrete questions from American national surveys conducted between 1949 and 1975, which implicated various values in diverse situations. Since the influence of education on each item is examined separately for each of four age cohorts, our detailed findings involve 600 sets of comparisons of values across a series of educational levels. As in the first study, which involved more than a thousand sets of comparisons of knowledge by educational levels, the presentation of such massive evidence creates a dilemma. Compression and condensation are essential to protect the reader from drowning in the ocean of data, but it is also essential to present enough detail to demonstrate the stability of the findings with replicated items and surveys and to show the variations in the patterning of effects on different values, in different situational contexts, for groups educated in different periods, and with aging.

We have chosen the same modes of presentation and the same tests and indexes of effect we employed in the first study. No one solution to the problems of presentation is ideal, perfectly satisfying both the need for detail and the need for compression and quick understanding. Any single index or statistical test gives some special vantage point for gauging effect but also has some special limitation. To prevent arbitrariness, several tests and indexes have been used and are incorporated into the tables. The lengthy tables, however formidable they appear, are a compromise arrived at after much thought. They provide for the interested reader a substantial portion, *but not all*, of the specific results from the analysis of each of the discrete items. Whatever the disadvantages of this mode of presentation, whatever the limitations of the various indexes employed, the advantage is that effects on knowledge and effects on values have been evaluated by the same procedures, subjected to the same tests, and measured against the same standards. Thus one can readily compare the relative effectiveness of education in the two realms. Summary measures have also been computed and are incorporated into the tables, whenever appropriate, for batteries of items that are homogeneous in content, helping the reader to inspect and comprehend the many pages of details.

In these surveys educational attainment was generally classified in terms of seven fairly refined categories. In one survey, the code provided for only five categories; in several others the classification was so refined that eight or nine categories are distinguishable; in four the exact number of years of education is specified. In our analysis, those who completed high school or college are *always* distinguished from those who did not complete the stage, and apart from the rare exceptions noted in the tables, those who completed eight years of elementary school are distinguished from those with fewer years of schooling. Those with *no* schooling at all are eliminated from almost all our analyses except the occasional surveys—too few to cause worry—where the original coding did not permit such refinement. At we stressed in our earlier book, this completely disadvantaged group has been so small a component of the white population of the United States during the periods studied that mixing them with those who had some schooling (where this had to be done) adds very little error to the descriptions of those with some elementary school.[1] At higher levels of education, although the refinement of the coding in some of the surveys would have permitted differentiation, we included those who had some vocational or trade school in addition to regular high school with the group of "graduates," and we treated those who had professional or graduate training in addition to college as "college graduates." Thus these two groups may in fact reflect the effects of the additional training some of their members received. But, apart from the occasional exceptions noted, the elementary-school "graduates" have had the full benefit of no less than eight years of education, and the least-educated group in the analyses has had at least some schooling.

The measurement of values, or of knowledge in the first study, rarely required such refinement. On most questions the respondent had a choice between two simple answers, one indicating support of the "good" value implicated in the situation, the other its rejection or the endorsement of the "bad" value. However, a third answer, "don't know," was permitted and coded. In our earlier study this feature created no perplexity. Although the lack of knowledge could take two different forms—*ignorance*, as revealed by answering "don't know" to a question of fact, or *misinformation* by venturing a definite, but incorrect answer, in both cases, the respondent clearly could be scored as not knowledgeable. In the current study, the "don't know" or undecided answer does create some perplexity. Though the respondent has not categorically endorsed the "good" value, neither has he rejected it completely or categorically endorsed the alternative "bad" value. He appears to be wavering, indecisive, conflicted—a reasonable and normal position for individuals confronting complex decisions involving a variety of considerations, where fully supporting one value may require sacrificing something else that is also desirable. Respondents who took such qualified, ambivalent positions are always included in our analyses and in effect assigned an intermediate score.[2] They are not counted as exhibiting the "good" value, but in the matrix from which the various indexes of effects of education are computed they are not lumped with those who have rejected the good value and thrown their full support behind the "bad" value.

Some may jump to the conclusion that our assessment is in error because these cases are misclassified. Had they been scored at one extreme or the other, depending on whether they were more or less educated we might have drawn an even more positive or more negative conclusion about the effects of education. Some might even argue that the wisest position when facing such conflicts of values is compromise or moderation—to reserve judgment and not be categorical. Others might argue that halfhearted support for good is no support at all. Our scoring convention seems to us the reasonable interpretation and a conservative practice. We neither add too much to the credit of education nor subtract too much. Fortunately, any misclassifications can create very little error, since only a very small proportion—generally less than 5% —of the samples answered "don't know" to most of our questions. And since such undecided respondents are not found consistently among either the more or the less educated, as revealed by careful inspection of the matrix on each item, whatever errors have been made are balanced out.[3] On any particular item where the problem appears to be of a magnitude and character to deserve attention, it will be noted.

In the tables of basic findings (Appendix C), the first three columns show the prevalence of support for the value implicated in each discrete question among the college graduates, high-school graduates, and elementary-school graduates within the specified age-group and birth cohort. This mode of presentation furnishes the reader much, but not all, of the richness and descriptive detail of the findings. If we had presented such findings for the six or seven levels of education distinguished in the surveys, we would truly have confronted him with an enormous task. If one must choose, it seems more important to show the benefits derived by those who have had the full course at each level. The elementary-school group provides a baseline for assessing the gains from secondary and higher education. By using only graduates, we address the question of the *maximum* enduring effects yielded by those educational experiences.

The figures in parentheses are the bases or numbers of cases used to compute each of the percentages. The reader, of course, will note that the base for estimating prevalence on a discrete item in particular groups is small; this is especially true of the highly educated in the oldest cohort and the least educated in the youngest cohort. However, the replications presented throughout the tables reinforce most conclusions, though occasionally they may leave us in doubt.

The two other modes for testing the effects and presenting the findings are shown in the last two columns of the tables in Appendix C. They compensate for the previous omission of some levels of education but also compress the findings radically. Using the maximum refinement permitted in the particular survey, we tested the relationship between education, over its full range of six levels, and the level of support of the value, as scored over the full range of alternative answers. This relationship is summarized by the two statistics shown. A chi-square (X^2) test indicates the significance of the difference. The symbols used are "ns" (not significant) when the chi-square value does not reach the .05 level, one asterisk when it reaches .05 but not .01, two asterisks when it reaches .01 but not .001, and three asterisks when it reaches or exceeds the .001 level. In making 600 tests, any investigation is bound to find a *few* instances where the differences are so big that they would occur by chance only once in a hundred times, but we have a *great many* tests where such large differences would occur by chance only once in a hundred times or even once in a thousand times. The reader can quickly establish the level of consistency by scanning the column of symbols in the various tables. The symbol "ns" obscures the fact that the chi-square test of the effect of education on a particular item sometimes comes very close to reaching significance. We do not try to make too much out of such discrete findings, and so we evaluate and present each one as "not significant." But since many discrete findings are independent tests of the same hypothesis, based on the very question repeated in another survey or on a series of indicators of the same value from separate surveys, a legitimate overall test made by combining several nearly significant chi-squares, or occasional nonsignificant tests with many significant ones, would have yielded highly significant results. This column in the tables therefore presents a highly conservative picture of the effects of education.[4] In the text, we will periodically report instances where the combination of chi-squares would lead to a revised and more positive conclusion about the effects of education.

The chi-square test by itself gives no indication of the magnitude or direction of the differences across all the educational levels. This information is provided in the last column of the tables, where we enter the *gamma* (γ), a coefficient of association developed especially for ordinal variables computed for each item over the full range and all the refined levels of education. We shall review this in more detail later, but the reader can see from the first three columns that although the relationships often are not linear, the prevalence of "good" values usually increases as people move up the educational ladder. The gammas convey this; a negative sign indicating the reverse pattern and a coefficient close to zero indicate that the effect of education on that particular variable is negligible.[5]

All the findings, with one exception, are based on questions that implicate values in various concrete situations rather than on direct questions about the desirability of some abstractly stated, highly general pattern of conduct or goal. The one exception is a battery that asked the respondent to *rank* a set of generally stated items in order of their desirability. Such a complex instrument, as previously noted, is not vulnerable to the biases that may afflict a direct simple question where by his choice of answer the respondent can present himself in a good or bad light. These findings are replicated in two surveys from the 1970s, but since they are limited to the one period and based on only one such instrument, they do not have the power of our many other findings. We shall present and dispose of them first, before turning to the much richer and far more generalizable data from the great many questions of the other type.

Hierarchy of Values

Respondents were shown a list of thirteen desirable qualities and asked "which three [were] the most desirable for a child to have." We used only seven of the qualities as criterion measures, selecting these "blindly"—with no knowledge of their relationship to education. These seven were chosen because they represent three contrasted clusters of values. The proper location of two of these clusters in the hierarchy of desirability seems unambiguous, and the third cluster is of special interest.[6]

Table C.1 (Appendix C) presents the replicated results for each of the four age-groups or birth cohorts, using the standard format and the several tests of the enduring effects of education employed throughout our study. The voluminous data may seem confusing at first, but the clarity and consistency in the replicated findings becomes evident as soon as we note the several dimensions implicit in the items. Items 1 and 2, "being considerate" and "being responsible," in contrast with items 6 and 7, "being neat and clean" and "having good manners," recall the old distinction between *morals* and *manners*. There is nothing bad or wrong about any of these qualities; but to elevate the latter pair to high rank in such a hierarchy is surely to place too great a value on the superficial. To elevate the former pair is to show a proper concern for the moral foundations of conduct.

Inspecting the first three columns in the table, we see that high-school graduates are somewhat more likely and college graduates far more likely than elementary-school graduates to regard these moral values as ranking high in importance. By contrast, items 6 and 7, especially "good manners," are far more likely to be given elevated rank by the least educated and are least likely to be elevated by the college graduates, though there are occasional inversions in the pattern. The pattern is stable in the two surveys, is characteristic of all age-groups, and persists up to age seventy-two. Inspection of the last column of the table shows that the sign of the gamma is positive in all sixteen tests in the sphere of morals and, by contrast, is *negative* in all sixteen tests in the sphere of manners. The magnitude of the coefficients, though not high, is not insubstantial. With too few exceptions to worry about, the chi-squares in the former sphere are significant. In the latter sphere, especially on item 7 and taking account of the combined results, the findings are significant for the three younger groups and up to age sixty. For those over sixty, the tests are not significant. It must be stressed that throughout this and the earlier study the much smaller size of the sample of the very old and the very small size of some of the cells among them may account for the more frequent nonsignificant chi-squares. However, the gammas provide another source of evidence on the pattern among the very old, and if they are positive and of magnitude similar to those for other age groups, they protect us from jumping too quickly to negative conclusions about effects among the very old.

Thus far education seems to have enduring effects in establishing a good hierarchy of values—in placing morals and manners in their proper places. Yet the evidence when we turn to item 5 in the table, "honesty," may seem contradictory. Certainly, honesty is a virtue, and it should be valued highly by all who are concerned with morals. The first three columns clearly show that one does not need much education to learn to put honesty in its proper high place. In five of the comparisons the high-school graduates are the most likely to rank it highly, and in the other three the elementary-school graduates are the most likely.

The finding is not surprising, and from one point of view is not contradictory. Honesty is such an obvious and old-fashioned virtue that anyone can learn to value it without benefit of formal education. In fact, across the nation in both surveys, honesty was placed among the three most desirable qualities more frequently than any of the other *twelve* qualities and, on the further probe, it was far and away most frequently described as the "most desirable of all" the qualities. Inspection of the table will show that among college graduates, too, honesty is more likely to be ranked among the top three than are being considerate or responsible. The lesser educated are more likely to give honesty high rank simply because for them it is *preeminent*, whereas among the highly educated it is *sometimes* pushed out of high place in the hierarchy by other values regarded as equally or more important. In no sense does it mean that the highly educated regard it as *unimportant*. In fact, only one solitary college graduate in the 1973 survey ranked it as one of the three least important qualities, and in the 1975 survey only two college graduates responded in that fashion. If one examines the pattern over all the refined levels of education, one can see in the last column that the signs vary and the relationship of education to the ranking of honesty is not statistically significant in half the tests. In the significant instances, the gammas are low, suggesting little or no relationship.

The cluster of values represented by items 3 and 4 were included to test whether *intellectual* values become elevated among those who have the benefit of more education. Our view was not that qualities of mind should take precedence over qualities of character in the hierarchy of values; although their proper placement is moot, our own curiosity led us to test this hypothesis. According high rank to the intellect is more prevalent among the educated, and with one exception the sign of the gamma is positive. But a few of the coefficients are close to zero, and the chi-squares are predominantly nonsignificant.[7] This set of findings is surely ironic and interesting, but judges might well differ as to its importance.[8]

We shall not extend this analysis of the hierarchy of values by presenting findings involving controls on other social factors. At best the findings are limited, referring only to one time period and based only on one very special instrument of measurement. They certainly suggest that education has enduring good effects,[9] but we shall reserve judgment until we examine the very large body of evidence based on many different questions covering a wide range of values and a long span of time. By now the reader is familiar with the standard format and character of the tables, and we turn to that evidence.

Values relating to Civil Liberties

Within the broad sphere of values relating to civil liberties, the many questions cover a variety of situations within which the issue of the liberties of different types of individuals is explored. We turn first to a large set of items that provide the most demanding tests of the support of these values.

Civil Liberties for Nonconformists and Freedom of Information

Table C.2.1 presents evidence from the early 1950s, based on seventeen questions about socialists, atheists, and communists. In items 1–6, however, the individuals were not labeled but were described as "somebody who is against all churches and religions" and as "a person who favors government ownership of all the railroads and all big industries" (see Appendix A for complete wording), so as to reduce ambiguity about the exact type of nonconformity and to eliminate the biases that might arise from an inflammatory symbol. The term "communist" was used throughout items 7–15 and in item 17, with various modifiers like "admitted" and "member" added to give specificity and to introduce shades of meaning, thus testing whether all respondents or certain educational subgroups take special note of the finer distinctions and apply the value differentially.

Subsets of questions (e.g., 1–3, 4–6) refer to the very same nonconformist but vary the situation within which his liberty is at issue, thus providing another test of whether the value is applied differentially. All the situations, however, place the nonconformist in the role of *communicator* — writer, teacher, speechmaker—and thus implicate *two* values. A restraint on the actor's liberty in turn reduces his audience's freedom to obtain the information he would have communicated.[10] The observed variation in the liberty allowed the same nonconformist when different audiences are exposed to his messages clearly warrants the inference that the respondents have indeed weighed the value of freedom of information and, perhaps in the spirit of protecting a particular audience, are willing to infringe its freedom.[11] By contrast, some of the items in the surveys of the later period, for example whether an atheist should be allowed to *vote*, do not implicate anyone else's freedoms and are pure measures of support for the value of liberty for the nonconformist.

The findings in the first three columns, when summarized for items 1–9, show that support of the two values implicated is least characteristic of the elementary-school group, somewhat more prevalent among the high-school graduates, and much more prevalent among the college graduates. Within the youngest cohort, on the average, the prevalence of support has increased by more than 40 percentage points. The effect of education diminishes regularly and dramatically with age, but even among the very old there is a substantial average increase of more than 20 percentage points in the prevalence of the value among the college graduates compared with the least-educated group among their age-mates.[12] Since the contrasted age-groups represent different birth cohorts, educated and developing in different historical periods, we must reserve final judgment on whether *aging* does in fact erode some of the earlier effects of education until we examine the cohort analyses and comparative findings for later periods. It is conceivable that the pattern observed in this particular generation of aged individuals reflects peculiarities in their rearing and education. One might have obtained the same findings if their values had been measured earlier, long before they became aged.[13] The tentative and *conservative* conclusion is that some of the good effects of education in inculcating these values do wither with age, but clearly a substantial part endures.

Inspection of the percentages for each of the discrete items 1–9 shows a striking consistency in the patterns. Up to age fifty, prevalence of support for the values rises regularly and dramatically with education in all nine tests. In the two older age groups, the differences are smaller and there are occasional inversions in the pattern, but the differences persist on most of the items right up to very old age and are still substantial in magnitude. The statistics in the last two columns show that the pattern is consistent over the full range of education. The chi-squares for ages up to fifty are uniformly and highly significant (with one exception out of 18 tests); the gammas are always positive and are generally of fairly high magnitude, with the exception of two special situations to be noted below. In the two older age groups, the results are usually significant and the gammas positive, but there are some nonsignificant results, one gamma of negative sign, and quite a number close to zero. The gammas usually decline in magnitude with age.

The consistency of the patterns with increasing age and education does not mean that individuals perceive the different kinds of nonconformists in the different situations in exactly the same light. Indeed, everyone—young or old, lowly or highly educated—differentiates sharply between circumstances in which they would apply or deny the values. In their eyes, the atheist is less entitled to his liberties than the socialist, and the admitted communist deserves them least of all. Especially when any of the nonconformists might take on the role of teacher, his liberties shall be denied.[14] Indeed, all the inversions, nonsignificant results, and negative gammas occur in these particular circumstances. It is ironic that even the highly educated, whose experience might have led them to prize academic freedom and the opportunity for college students to learn everything, very rarely apply their values to these particular circumstances. Had we eliminated these special items, the effects of education in the very old would have been much larger and longer enduring. Including these items works to make the overall conclusion conservative. Clearly, neither the lesser nor the better educated apply their values indiscriminately, and the very old seem to make the sharpest distinctions of all.[15]

The remaining items in table C.2.1 enlarge the body of evidence, reveal the same basic findings, and show some additional subtleties and occasional blemishes on the pattern of good effects of education. The nonconformist in items 10–12, decribed in abbreviated form in the table as a "suspected communist," is, in the detailed wording of the question from the Stouffer survey of 1954, someone who has sworn "under oath that he has never been a communist" but his "loyalty has been questioned before a congressional committee." Surely he is different from the "admitted communist" described in items 7–9 and implicated in the same three situations. By reasonable standards and taken at face value, he is innocent of nonconformity. The summary findings for items 10–12 juxtaposed to the summary findings for items 7–9 show that all individuals—young and old, more and less educated—make a sharp distinction and extend him far more liberties. And the taint of suspicion, when unfounded, does *not* deter the oldest college graduates from applying the value. There is no decline in effect with age. But the analysis of these discrete items over the *full range* of education does show among the very old that the findings are nonsignificant—that the gammas decline in magnitude. And when an accused communist is cast in the role of *teacher*, the mere accusation washes out the effect of education among the very old, yielding a gamma of zero.

Items 13–15 are drawn from Gallup polls rather than from NORC surveys, but the basic findings are the same. Item 14, asked in 1953, underscores the present purity of the individual by its redundancy: "former members of the Communist Party who have resigned from the party." Nevertheless, as the chi-squares and gammas reveal, the more educated among the *middle-aged* as well as the very old are no more likely than the less educated to apply the value when the former nonconformist is cast in the role of *teacher*.

Items 16 and 17 in the table show the replicated findings for two questions, repeated in surveys separated by several years during which the climate of opinion was changing. Strictly speaking, the second survey does not represent the early 1950s, since it was conducted in 1957, but the longer interval between measurements creates a more incisive test of the stability of the findings.[16] The better educated are consistently more likely to apply libertarian values. These effects endure, the major exception once again being among the very old, where the 1954 tests show not only an inversion, but also a negative gamma and a nonsignificant chi-square.

The early 1950s, of course, were the period of McCarthyism, and some of the surveys were conducted at the very time, 1953–54, when the senator was at the height of his activities and power. Naturally, everyone was responding in some degree to that current experience as well as reflecting his past educational experiences. But since the situation was constant, the findings can reveal still the *differential* response of various educational and age groupings to that very special stimulus. The findings must be seen in that context, and as we examine similar data for later periods, we shall see whether the effects observed are greater or smaller, and whether they are generalizable. Surely that was the most trying of times for libertarians, and table C.1 therefore presents the most demanding tests and the most compelling evidence of the good and enduring effects of education in strengthening the values of civil liberties.

Table C.2.2 presents parallel findings from the 1960s, based on seven items contained within two surveys. The first two items again implicate the value of freedom of information for the audience as well as the value of civil liberties for a nonconformist. They are very similar in content and wording to items 2 and 3 in table C.2.1 and, as before, refer to an atheist without invoking that emotional term or label, simply stating that he "admitted in public that he did not believe in God." That the audience implicated in new question 2, "high-school" students, is younger and presumably needs more protection than the college students implicated in the earlier question makes more compelling the new finding of the greater support for liberty among the educated. As the atmosphere changed, support for the values increased dramatically in all segments of the population—young and old, more and less educated. Since the contemporary climate was a constant, impinging on everyone, the new comparisons can reveal the effects of the amount and kind of education this set of birth cohorts received when they entered the schools and colleges a decade later than the earlier set of cohorts and can determine whether the effects endured up to specified stages of aging.

As in the earlier period, on items 1 and 2 education substantially increases the prevalence of support for the values, but the differences once again diminish among the old, especially when the atheist is cast as a *teacher*, where the findings are nonsignificant. Two new items, 3 and 4, show good and long-enduring effects of education in increasing support of the value of civil liberties for an atheist, the differences being large and significant even among the very old. The summary findings for the battery of four items referring to an atheist show that the prevalence of the value increases by more than 50 percentage points, on the average, among the young and by about 30 percentage points among the very old.

A new battery, items 5–7, reveals some of the subtle ways education affects the application of the value of civil liberties. All the groups, no matter what their age or education, regarded members of the Communist party or the Ku Klux Klan or prisoners as less deserving of the right to vote than an atheist. The effects of education are dampened. Nevertheless, *averaging* the findings shows that the more educated are considerably more likely to apply the value of liberty to such special cases and extremist groups. The differences between the levels are smaller but are still substantial among the very old. When the discrete items are examined, however, the more educated manifest a distinctive pattern in the way they apply their usual libertarian values. They are more supportive of extending the right to vote to members of the Communist party and the Ku Klux Klan, although as usual the differences diminish

35

sharply among the very old. But for prisoners the more educated reverse their usual stance and are more in favor of *curtailing* the right. Whether this represents a sensible distinction or an inappropriate and discriminatory one, blemishing or spoiling the larger pattern of good and enduring effects of education, the reader must decide. Since we will present additional data bearing on such distinctive patterns, one should postpone final judgment.

Table C.2.3 presents parallel findings for the 1970s.[17] Items 1–9 are the very same questions asked by NORC in 1954 and again in 1972 and 1974. The same instruments employed by the same agency in surveys separated by twenty years insure a thorough and rigorous test of whether the effects of education on the values of civil liberty and freedom of information, as applied to the wide range of situations, are uniform across and generalizable to different generations and cycles of education. Following cohorts as they age by means of these comparable surveys and measurements separated by twenty years will provide direct and powerful evidence that can either strengthen or weaken our tentative conclusions about aging. And the general stability of the replicated findings from 1972 and 1974, with the exception of certain discrete findings among the *very old*, establishes that the net effect of sampling and measurement error and of transient conditions at the times of the two inquiries is very small and gives us safe grounds for concluding that any major changes observed in the recent period are not artifacts.

The reliability of the findings for the 1950s is equally critical to such conclusions. The stable findings from the two simultaneous, equivalent surveys conducted by the Gallup Poll and by NORC that composed the larger Stouffer inquiry are presented in table C.2.4. With the exception of certain discrete findings among the oldest cohort, they establish that the net effect not only of sampling and measurement error but also of whatever distinctive practices the particular agencies employed is very small. We turn with confidence first to the basic findings for the 1970s, then to their comparison with the 1950 findings.

In every one of the nine situations, the effects of education, twice tested, are found to be large and enduring in all the groups up to age sixty. Almost always, the prevalence of support increases regularly and dramatically as one moves through the three major levels of education; the chi-squares in all but one of the fifty-four tests involved are significant, and the combined test on that item would have been significant; the gammas are always positive and substantial in magnitude and rarely diminish with aging. This does not mean that the educated apply their values indiscriminately. As was true in the earlier periods, all the groups—the less educated as well as the more educated, the younger and the older—differentiate between situations where the values are more and less applicable, once again making the sharpest separation in situations where the nonconformist is cast in the role of *teacher*. Indeed, the two instances out of fifty-four where either the effects of education are nonsignificant or the gamma approximates zero involve these special situations.

Among those over age sixty, the prevalence of support for the values usually increases regularly and substantially as one moves across the three major levels of education, but there are a good many instances where findings from the replications are contradictory as well as several nonsignificant tests. The gammas usually are substantial and of about the same magnitude as in the younger cohorts, but there are several instances where the gammas have diminished sharply—notably in situations where the nonconformist is a teacher.

From the many tests it seems reasonable to conclude that the effects of education on these values are large and lasting and to some extent endure into very old age. If we look at the summary findings for items 1–9 presented in the table, which averages out the irregularities on occasional items and replications, prevalence of support rises by 35–45 percentage points as one moves from the least to the most educated members in all four cohorts. It is also clear from the summary data, looking down each column, that prevalence of the value declines when one compares older individuals with younger ones of the *same* educational level. Aging *as such* thus seems to have a depressing effect on the value, but this process in no way destroys the effects of education. Since the decline occurs among the older at all three levels of education, the *difference* between the levels is preserved and persists even among the very old.[18]

As we noted in discussing similar findings for the 1950s, one must be cautious in concluding from one such analysis that aging has a depressing effect. Once again let us stress that the older group in table C.2.3 is not the same cohort as the younger group, measured at a later stage of life. They are a different generation, and their lesser support of the values may reflect particular educational and other experiences during their development rather than their aging. But since that decline also characterized the older groups in the 1950s, especially their more educated members, as well as the older groups in the 1970s—generations separated by twenty years—it seems unreasonable to try to explain away the decline with aging as due to the peculiar experience of a particular generation. By juxtaposing the summary findings for items 1–9 in table C.2.1 and table C.2.3 we can observe the uniformity of the process: in the 1950s, the marked decline with aging occurred essentially among the better educated. (The least educated among the young started out so close to the floor that very little further decline in the values could set in with aging.) We should withhold final judgment until we make more precise analyses based on exactly comparable age-groupings, take account of floor and ceiling effects, and trace specific cohorts as they age. Tentatively the conservative conclusion is that some of the effects of education on these values decline with aging, but a substantial portion endures far into old age.[19]

Tables C.2.5–6 present a series of refined comparisons, all strictly comparable in their definition of the age and educational categories and in the survey agency involved, that will permit more precise examination of the uniformity of the effects of the education gained in different historical periods and of their persistence or decline with aging. In table C.2.5, each tier shows a pair of generations that have reached the same age but that were educated in different historical periods. For example, in the first tier, all respondents have reached ages thirty to thirty-nine, but the two generations were born twenty years apart. To be sure, to catch different birth cohorts or generations when they have reached the same age, the measurements must be made at different times, and the different circumstances at the times of measurement may have influenced the responses. But fortunately this has not obscured the findings and can be taken into account.

The top half of the table shows the prevalence of support over the battery of nine items on civil liberties and freedom of information. In each of the four pairs of comparisons, the individuals, although of constant age, represent generations who developed and were schooled in different historical periods. Yet the effect of education, whatever its kind, is to increase the prevalence of support by almost the exact amount in three of the four pairs of comparisons. Whichever two generations are examined, the effects become smaller when we examine individuals who have reached older ages; but they surely are substantial even in the oldest age groups examined.[20]

These conclusions, however, are based on the increased prevalence of the value, expressed in *absolute* terms. The later generation in each of the contrasted pairs was measured in 1974, when support of the value had become much more widespread than in 1954, even among the least educated. Some might argue that the equal percentages do not mean equal effects, when the baselines from which the gains are measured are so different for the two generations. In one respect it is *more* difficult for the most educated in the *later* generation to show a gain, since the least educated score closer to the ceiling. For example, if the value were prevalent among 80% of the elementary-school group, the maximum possible gain from further education would be only 20%, and an observed increase of ten percentage points would be half, or 50%, of the possible gain. By contrast, if only 20% of the least educated exhibited the value, gains of as much as 80% could be registered. In this instance an observed increase of the same absolute size, ten percentage points, would only be one-eighth, or 12.5%, of the possible maximum gain.

By this logic and this index, gains of any given magnitude—even very small ones—deserve and are given greater weight when the baseline is high; that is, when the good value is common among the least educated. But to see the matter this way is to pay attention only to the technical or mathematical implications of the high baseline and to ignore its meaning. When the good value is common, anyone who exhibits it is, in a way, simply floating with the tide, being carried along by the prevailing winds of doctrine. Therefore, when the baseline is high, though it may be difficult to register a large gain among the educated, it is certainly not difficult for them to maintain or express the value.[21] Why give gains under such conditions any added weight by transforming the percentages?

By contrast, when the value is uncommon, someone who exhibits it is, in a sense, swimming against strong countercurrents—surely a difficult task. To allow that the gain expressed in absolute percentage points under these conditions when the baseline is low can be a large and impressive number seems only fair. In times when it is difficult to maintain and express a cherished value, any gains produced by education deserve special weight. Why discount them by transforming the absolute percentages? We are inclined for these reasons to regard the absolute gain as the more meaningful index of the effects of education. For those who prefer an index of effects adjusted in terms of the different baselines and distances to the ceiling of the contrasted generations, the last column of table C.2.5 provides such an index. Although that index suggests that effects are not equal, it does show that they are substantial no matter which generation is examined, even in the very oldest pair of age groups, although once again there is a decline at that stage.

The bottom half of table C.2.5 compares pairs of contrasted generations, equated in age but separated by a ten-year interval. The measure of effects is the one item about an atheist common to the 1964 and 1974 NORC surveys, the points when the generations were measured. Whichever index is examined, the effects of the education these generations experienced is about equal up to a fairly advanced age, but among the very old—whichever generation they represent—the effects, though substantial, have declined.

Table C.2.6 rearranges the data from the 1954 and 1974 surveys to show the changes in effect as contrasted educational levels age over the twenty-year interval. Two cohorts or generations are tracked through time, the later generation being traced up to age fifty-nine and the earlier up to age sixty-nine. In both instances, of course, the aging has occurred during a particular historical period, and the second measurement was made in the context of the events of 1974. But the historical context is a constant for everyone and does not obscure the comparison between educational levels and the examination of the *differential* changes as the more and less educated have aged and experienced the events of those twenty years. The summary at the bottom of the table, which compresses the findings and averages out the irregularities over the nine discrete items, shows for the more recent generation, those aged thirty to thirty-nine in 1954, that the differences have remained intact up to age fifty-nine. The prevalence of the value increased among the least educated members of this cohort but also increased among the more educated, and the distance between them has not diminished at all. Within the earlier cohort, those already aged forty to forty-nine in 1954, the educational levels have become a bit more alike by age sixty to sixty-nine, but the distance between them is still substantial.

The detailed findings for each discrete item show not only changes in the *prevalence* of the value with aging of the three major educational subgroups within each cohort, but also changes with aging in the significance of the effects and in the gamma over the *full range* and all refined levels of education. Whatever minor changes have occurred in the prevalence of the value or in the significance of the differences or magnitude of the gammas as these cohorts and the subgroups within them have aged, considering the combined evidence, the effects of education on most of the items have persisted. The only totally negative finding occurs, once again, when a nonconformist—a "socialist"—is cast in the role of teacher. By the time the earlier cohort has reached age sixty to sixty-nine, there is no longer any difference in the prevalence of support, the chi-square is nonsignificant, and the gamma is effectively zero.

These many tests of different types surely provide dramatic and consistent evidence that education has large and lasting effects in increasing support of civil liberties for nonconformists and freedom of information. The skeptic might accept the findings but question our conclusion that education has enduring effects on *values*. He might argue that the answers to such a battery of questions are simply indicative of *self- or group interest*. For example, if the educated are more secular or nonreligious than the less educated and if, for the sake of the argument, we assume that they themselves are more radical than the less educated, then they are merely expressing selfish support for their own liberties and for those who think like them rather than any high-minded, unselfish ideal that liberty is to be valued for its own sake. He might assert that the small changes with aging do not signify any decline in the *value*. The young presumably are more radical than the old, and the differences in support of the liberties involved once again simply reflect the respective interests and ideologies of the young and the old.

Table C.2.7 should allay any such skepticism. In a series of tests, each one duplicated in surveys from different time periods, 1954, 1964, and 1974, the effects of education are examined for groups contrasted in education but equated in their personal sympathies or beliefs. For example, in the first row of the table, one notes that in 1974, among frequent churchgoers, the willingness to allow a speech *against* religion is 39% more prevalent among the most educated than among the least educated; the differences being highly significant and the gamma fairly high. Even in 1954, in the days of McCarthyism, among those who believed communism was a "very great danger," the prevalence of support for a speech against private ownership increased by 41% as one moved from the least to the most educated.

The consistent evidence from this long series of compelling tests is that education greatly increases support of the value even when it demands that individuals oppose their own sympathies. There are only two instances in the thirty-six comparisons where the combined evidence from the three statistical tests is thoroughly negative; both are in 1954, and again the socialist or communist is cast as a teacher.

Civil Liberties and Due Process of Law for Extremists and Deviants

Findings from a brief battery of questions asked in the 1960s, reviewed earlier, had indicated that the educated were more supportive of the right to vote for members of the Communist party and the Ku Klux Klan. However, everyone was less inclined to apply libertarian values to these extremist groups than to the other types of nonconformists, and the effects of education were dampened and diminished among the very old. In the special case of *prisoners*, the findings took the reverse pattern, the more educated being even *less* supportive of their right to vote than the less educated. Findings from five other questions asked in the 1970s, items 10–14 in table C.2.3, not previously reviewed, strengthen the evidence and cast doubt on the earlier, rather anomalous variation in the usual pattern of effects of education on such values.

Three of the items deal with the liberties of "radical groups": whether the authorities shall be permitted to search their meeting places without a warrant, spy on their members even though they have not broken the law, or deny them bail and imprison them if they are suspected of inciting a riot. On the average, as the summary shows, and on each of the three items the more educated are much more likely to support the liberties of radicals and protect their rights to due process, but, as before, the differences diminish among the very old and are not significant.

The comparative findings for two questions on whether the police should be permitted to search the home of a *criminal* suspect without warrant and to imprison him without bail (items 13 and 14) test whether the more educated discriminate against criminals and reverse their normal pattern of support of the values involved. Among the old, education has little or no effect, but up to age fifty, and perhaps beyond that stage, the effects of education are certainly positive. The earlier anomalous finding from the one item on prisoners' right to vote asked in the 1960s thus seems a limited aberration and, at worst, depending on one's judgment, a minor flaw in the pattern of good and fairly long-lasting effects.[22]

Liberty for Public Expression

One final battery of four questions tests the effects of education on values relating to civil liberties in a quite different context. These deal with the rights of members of the *general public*, rather than nonconformists, to express themselves in various ways in an attempt to influence governmental decisions. Three of the items fall within the realm of traditional, conventional acts, ranging from criticizing a decision supported by the majority through circulating petitions, to "holding peaceful demonstrations"; the fourth item is in sharp contrast and asks whether "people should be allowed to block the entrance to a government building for a period of time."

As table C.2.8 reveals, on the average and for each item 1–3, when such liberties take a conventional form, support increases substantially and significantly among the more educated, though the effects are smaller and occasionally not significant among the very old. But when the value is applied in the service of the unconventional, extreme act of blocking a building entrance, the pattern is sharply different, as is shown in item 4 in the table. In 1971 hardly anyone—young or old, more or less educated, supported such liberties. The differences between educational groups are not significant, but the gammas computed over the full range of education show that education in fact has an *inverse* effect. This reversal of the general pattern surely shows that education does not lead to an indiscriminate endorsement of all kinds of liberties. Some may weigh the finding differently, arguing that by this acid test the educated have faltered and fallen short of full support of the value of civil liberties. Unfortunately, these data were available only for the one survey in the 1970s, and there is no evidence on the uniformity and generalizability of this particular pattern in other periods and for other generations.

Controls on Other Factors

These many positive findings, showing large differences between educational groups that endure even into old age, should not be accepted as evidence of the effects of education on these values until we control other major factors and find that the differences persist. On every one of these items, as we noted in chapter 1, we have controlled the series of antecedent variables found to be the major social determinants of educational attainment, which might thus have accounted for the values, then reexamined the differences between educational groups. The findings on values relating to civil liberties are presented in table D.1 in Appendix D. In this and in the later tables that relate to other values, the top section summarizes the results of all the discrete tests where the contrasted educational groups were equated on each of six antecedent factors—sex, ethnicity, and social, residential, regional, and religious origins.[23]

And as we also noted in chapter 1, two other major determinants of educational attainment—race and birth cohort—were automatically controlled by the basic procedures routinely employed in all the initial analyses of the effects of education. In the initial analyses of the surveys from the 1970s, the factor of ethnicity was also automatically controlled because about 97% of the white respondents were native-born. Since the contrasted educational groups were almost completely homogeneous in this respect to start with, there was no need for any special control over the variable in the tests from this period. Thus, in the twenty-one tests of the effect of education on civil liberties values in the surveys from the 1970s, previously shown in table C.2.3, the positive findings on every test for individuals up to age sixty cannot be accounted for by nativity, since that variable was already under control. On top of that, add the dramatic finding summarized in table D.1, that in all fifteen tests specially conducted among individuals who were uniformly of native birth, the differences in values among educational groups remained significant and the gamma was substantial. This grand total of thirty-six tests not only protects us from spurious conclusions about the effects of education but also insures that we are examining the effects of *American* education.[24] In reviewing the later tables in Appendix D, the reader should apply the same kind of reckoning to the totals entered under the variable of native birth.

The findings from the other long series of controlled tests, summarized in the top section of table D.1, also safeguard our tentative general conclusion about the positive effects of education on values relating to civil liberties. The differences persist in test after test, despite the many controls.[25] For example, among males the differences between educational groups remain significant on 51 out of the 53 items tapping these values. Among females, the differences persist on 49 of the items. The gammas on the average are substantial in magnitude for both males and females.

In focusing on the main question of whether the educational effects persist, the reader should not neglect the important question of whether the effects are *differentially* greater in certain social groups, which is also answered in these tables. Such a finding would specify the effects of education more precisely, perhaps circumscribe it, although it would in no way deny its good effects. There are many grounds for entertaining such hypotheses. As a result of their early socialization some groups might be more resistant to the value changes education might initiate, and in later life they might end up in milieus that are more or less conducive to maintaining the values education taught them. Or if higher educational institutions had been more selective in recruiting members from a particular group—for example, women—or if women were exposed to particular types of schools or colleges or subjected to different modes of instruction even when in the same institutions, the effects might well be differential. And since the careers of men and women have often taken different courses and the roles prescribed for them have been different— especially in the generations brought under scrutiny in our surveys—in later life the earlier effects of education might well be dampened for one sex and enhanced for the other.

However plausible this seems, there is relatively little evidence that education has differential effects between men and women. In both groups the effects are almost always significant, and the gammas on the average are of about the same magnitude. One may still argue that the *means* obscure subtle differences. The respective distributions of gammas, showing the effect for each discrete item, could be different and yet yield averages of the same magnitude. The findings from inspecting each of the gammas are also summarized in the table. In about two-thirds of the tests, the coefficients differ by less than .10. In the remaining instances, the higher gammas almost always characterize the men, suggesting a differentially greater effect of education, but the differential even then is not of great magnitude or very common.

The other findings presented in the top section of table D.1 provide little evidence of differential effects except for groups contrasted in religious origins.

The effects are more frequently significant among Protestants than among Catholics; the gamma on the average is higher in magnitude, and over many discrete tests more frequently of higher magnitude. More detailed inspection of the specific items establishes, however, that only in the surveys in the early 1950s did these differential effects occur. Since they characterized individuals of all ages, they cannot reflect the distinctive experiences or education of a particular generation of Catholics or Protestants. It seems that the atmosphere of that historical period somehow had a pervasive effect on Catholics and often diluted or washed out the usual effects of education in strengthening support of civil liberties, for reasons our inquiry cannot illuminate. Whatever the cause, over the much longer span of time examined, the effects of education among both Catholics and Protestants are generally positive and about equal in magnitude.

Having been alerted to the implications of the findings summarized in the top section of this table, the reader will be able to detect from the later tables in Appendix D whether differential effects are peculiar to certain value spheres and whether they occur consistently in certain of the various social groups described. We shall not dwell on the question but shall turn instead to the bottom section of this and later tables, which summarizes the findings when adults contrasted in their past educational attainments are equated on two features of their *current* situation.

These controls serve a different function from the controls on characteristics that are *antecedent* to education. When we control current social class or current residence in analyzing the effects of education, we are not protecting the findings from spuriousness. Current position, since it does not antedate education, therefore could not account for the original findings, except insofar as it reflects earlier regional or social origins. These controls test whether the effects of education endure only under certain conditions of later life. Educational credentials facilitate entry into privileged occupations or into marriages with the more privileged. When we compare adults who are all in relatively low class positions, we are testing whether the values of mature, educated adults can endure despite a fall to disadvantaged status. When we compare mature adults who are all in higher class positions, we are testing whether the less educated can learn particular values merely as a result of their ascent, then maintain them despite their previous educational disadvantage. As table D.1 reveals, there is clear evidence that the effects of education often are dissipated or weakened to some extent among individuals who have ended up in the blue-collar classes. Among those of higher status, the effects are substantial and generally significant.[26] Advantaged position thus helps maintain the earlier effects in this value sphere, but it cannot compensate for educational disadvantage, since the differences among those of contrasted education persist and are enhanced under such conditions.

Many of the values examined in this study—for example, racial equality—are not in conformity with the social norms that have prevailed in the South.

The controls on current residence therefore generally test whether the values inculcated by education can survive only when the milieu in later life is friendly to the value or whether they will be retained under conditions that are hostile; thus they are compelling indications of just how powerful a force education can be. These tests show that the effects of education on values relating to civil liberties are significant in almost all instances no matter what the region of residence, and there is no evidence for any differential effects relating to residence in the South or the North.

Freedom of Information

The earlier battery of questions dealing with the freedom of a nonconformist to act as a communicator—speechmaker, writer, teacher—also implicated the value of freedom of information. Each question, of course, specified a particular kind of audience, for example, college students rather than the general public, who would be free to receive a specified kind of controversial information, such as atheistic or socialistic. Although the effects of education were found to be pervasive, spread across the diversity of situations described, the findings also showed that the level and pattern of support for freedom of information depended on the audience and the information to be communicated.

Another question dealing with a different kind of information permits further exploration of the domain within which education affects the value of freedom of information and has the added advantage that it presents the issue in explicit and sharp terms and yields replicated evidence from several time periods. The question asks whether "birth control *information* should be available to *anyone* who wants it."[27] The findings presented in table C.3.1, when juxtaposed to the earlier findings of tables C.2.1–8, show that such information is regarded as far less dangerous than atheistic or radical ideas, and its dissemination is far less controversial. Even in earlier periods, very large majorities of the young and the old, the more and the less educated, favored making the information available. Those who greet these findings with skepticism or surprise should note that the question does not measure whether respondents themselves favor birth control, or want to encourage others to practice it, or want birth-control devices to be distributed, or want compulsory lectures on the topic to be given in high schools, but simply asks whether *information* should be available "to anyone who wants it." Since a preface informed the respondent that "in some places in the United States it is not legal to supply birth control information," the question measures specifically the support for people's being freed from the restraints of law to obtain information if they seek it.

The combined evidence in table C.3.1 on the effects of education on this specific application of the value of freedom of information is equivocal. To be sure, in every one of the twenty tests, the gamma has a positive sign, and the value is more prevalent among the college-educated than among the elementary school group in eighteen of the twenty comparisons. But the replications often yield inconsistent findings, and the effects of education shown by the increasing prevalence or by the gammas or chi-squares are meager and not significant in a considerable number of the tests. For the moment, the conservative conclusion would be that education has little effect on this particular application of the value of freedom of information. Even if education did not have all-pervasive effects throughout the domain within which the value applies, that would not completely discredit education, and the gross findings presented thus far may be misleading. Almost everyone is in favor of freedom for this particular kind of information, and the high-school graduates had almost reached the ceiling of the instrument long ago. It may be an insensitive test, and it is far from a demanding one. The earlier findings in more controversial areas seem to us to provide more compelling evidence of the effects of education on the value.

Table C.3.2 shows clearly that the initial gross findings were misleading and demonstrates why. It reexamines the effects of education in all the time periods and replicated surveys, separately for Protestants and Catholics. Elsewhere in our analyses, religious affiliation and other variables are introduced as controls to check on the possibility that initially *positive* findings are spurious. Here the variable of religion is introduced to check on the possibility that initially *negligible* or modest findings are misleading. If the positive effects were dampened among Catholics, when the two religious groups were combined in the initial analysis, any large effects among Protestants would be offset and the aggregate findings would be modest or could even be negligible. This turns out to be true in all five surveys. Among Protestants the effects are uniformly significant and substantial. Among Catholics they are uniformly nonsignificant and small in magnitude, and in the earlier period the effects are inverse, with education working upon Catholics to produce a slight *decrease* in the value. Certainly this more refined analysis circumscribes these effects of education, limiting them mainly to those whose conception of the circumstances in which freedom of information should be applied was not shaped by Catholic doctrine. For such individuals, the effects are far larger than one would have realized from the initial findings. Some might conclude that education is not a powerful force in this special instance if it cannot modify a doctrinally fortified position. Others might argue that it is to education's credit that it did not undermine particular beliefs Catholics regarded as right.[28]

Controls on Other Social Factors

The findings summarized in table D.2 establish that the effects of education on this application of the value of the freedom of information persist when various social factors other than religion are controlled. The refined analysis by religion, just reviewed, establishes that the differences persist when the contrasted educational groups are matched in religion and are Protestant.

Freedom from Legal Constraints in Choosing to Intermarry

Table C.4.1 presents replicated findings in each of three time periods relating to the value of freedom of choice in personal and social relations, as applied to the special situation of whites and blacks who choose to intermarry. The question in the seven surveys used specifically asks whether individuals should be free to choose a partner of different race or should be prevented by law from exercising their preferences. Note that the question does not measure the respondent's (all of them white in our studies) own preferences in a partner or ask whether he would encourage others to choose or avoid such a partner or disapprove or approve of intermarriage. Just as the question in our last section dealt with individuals' freedom not to be hampered by the law in obtaining birth-control information—*if they want it*—here too the question deals only with individuals' freedom not to be hampered by law if they want to intermarry.[29]

When the Gallup Poll asked the question, a preface remarked, "some states have laws making it a crime for a white person and a Negro to marry," and the respondent who then indicated his opposition was in effect stating that he wished an already established law to be stricken from the statute book. The NORC version of the question did not carry any such prefatory information and simply asked whether "there should be laws against marriage between Negroes and whites." The stability of the results despite this important variation in the wording only makes the findings more compelling.

The effects of education throughout these tests are consistently large and significant and endure into old age, no matter what the time period or generation involved. Of the twenty-four tests presented in table C.4.1, all but one show a marked increase in prevalence of support of the value of freedom from constraints of law in such choices, with a significant chi-square and a sizable gamma.

That education has enduring effects on this application of the general value is shown even more clearly in table C.4.2, where two independent sets of tests, based on the surveys of the two agencies, show changes in the value as a series of cohorts are aged by a number of years into the 1970s, some aging up to their middle sixties. Despite the aging, substantial significant differences persist in every test, and the gammas generally remain as high in magnitude or *increase* with aging.

Controls on Other Factors

Table D.3 summarizes the findings on the effects of education on this value when a series of other factors were controlled. The effects persist in the face of all these controls. The differences between educational levels, matched on other factors, are consistently significant, and the gammas continue to be high. The conclusions are surely not spurious. That differences in support for individuals to opt for interracial marriage without legal constraints persist among individuals reared and now residing in the South—the site of such laws—suggests how powerful the effects of education are. Once again, as with values relating to civil liberties, there is considerable evidence that the effects of education are differentially greater and more frequently significant among adults in advantaged class positions. Such a situation helps maintain the effects of education but clearly does not counterbalance earlier educational disadvantage.

The Value of Privacy and Protection from Wiretapping

The findings from the various questions already reviewed indicate that education increases support of the values of liberty and freedom for many kinds of people in many—though not all—spheres and their protection from arbitrary laws. Table C.5 presents evidence on support for the value of privacy and for protection from legally instituted wiretapping, drawn from replicated surveys spanning a twenty-five-year period, thus measuring the effects of education for generations educated in contrasted times and subsequently surveyed in strikingly different historical contexts.[30] We know from other evidence that a majority of Americans during the 1950s regarded wiretapping as a legitimate institution to protect national security and that substantial support continued until about 1970. In the 1970s, after Watergate, a great many people became sensitive to the abuses of wiretapping and the dangers it presented to the value of privacy, and the climate of national opinion changed. As table C.5 reveals, in every group—young or old, more or less educated—there was a dramatic increase in opposition to wiretapping.[31] Did education sensitize individuals to the dangers of wiretapping before the flagrant abuses made the dangers obvious to all?

Ironically, the evidence of table C.5 consistently shows, *at best*, that education has had no effect on the value of privacy and protection from wiretapping, neither increasing nor decreasing its support. In every time period, the differences between the educational levels within each generation and at every age are almost always nonsignificant, the differences in prevalence of support for the value are negligible, and the gammas are very low in magnitude.

A depressing conclusion is suggested by the consistently *negative* signs of the gammas, for education seemingly *decreases* support for the value throughout this long span of time. This strange pattern was present even in the 1970s, when it might be construed as a perverse response to the invasion of privacy and the abuses of wiretapping.

Equality of Opportunity for Minorities

A series of questions repeated in surveys conducted both by NORC and by the Gallup Poll over a long span of time measured support of the value of equality as applied to the rights of several minorities to equal opportunity in the social, economic and political spheres. The reader can examine just how reliable and comprehensive the evidence is, and how far it can be generalized to different spheres, minorities and time periods.

Table C.6 shows the white support for equality of *economic* and *social* opportunity for blacks in surveys in the early and late 1960s. By the beginning of that decade, support of the value was already widespread, and the less-educated groups were relatively close to the ceiling on equality of economic opportunity and fairly close to the ceiling on social equality. By the end of the decade they had moved much closer to the ceiling on social equality. Although this limits the size of the effects that can be demonstrated, one nevertheless observes considerable increase in the prevalence of the value among the more educated and sees the difference between educational levels is as great among the older cohorts, whichever generation they represent, and endures into very old age.[32] The gammas are always positive and substantial in magnitude, and they do not decline with age. In light of the combined evidence, the occasional nonsignificant chi-squares, mainly in the very oldest group where the sample size is very small, should be given little weight.

Readers will note that the two questions fall within the broad domain covered by many studies of prejudice. But since they deal with the specific dimension of whether or not a minority should be subject to discriminatory treatment and worse, they implicate the value of equality. By contrast, other traditional areas of study in race relations, such as beliefs and stereotypes about minorities or feelings and preferences about intimacy, contact, or social distance in relation to minorities, cover important dimensions of prejudice but do *not* measure the value of equality or other values of concern to us. They are thus excluded from our studies.[33] Stember's findings indicate that respondents are not simply expressing their diffuse feelings and prejudices in answering our two questions; prejudiced individuals and those who find personal contact with minorities awkward or dislike it may nevertheless support equal rights. In surveys in the 1940s, support of the egalitarian view that employers should hire "the most capable people whether they are Jewish or not" increased markedly with education, 77% of the college group then favoring that policy. But the individual's own preferences about a worker who was Jewish were *unrelated* to education, and 44% of the college group stated that it would make a difference to them if a new employee were Jewish.[34]

Table C.7.1 presents findings for the late 1950s from a battery of questions on equality of political opportunity for various minorities. The question describes a candidate for the presidency who is a member of a minority group and always specifies that he is "well qualified" and nominated by the respondent's "own party." Rejection therefore reflects only the minority membership and represents a denial of equal opportunity. Support, however, represents more than just an endorsement of the *principle* of equality of opportunity. That could have been elicited by a simple question on whether a minority candidate should be allowed to run, parallel in form to questions in the economic and social realm that asked only whether minorities should have equal access to public facilities and jobs. This question goes beyond that. The respondents have to commit themselves to vote for the minority candidate, thus overriding any personal prejudices in order to act in terms of the value. Any positive findings should be regarded as compelling evidence of the effects of education.

Support cannot simply be the expression of self- or group interest in these analyses. Since blacks were excluded from all the samples, only whites are answering the questions about a black candidate. Jews are such a tiny component of all the samples that their inclusion cannot affect the findings on the Jewish candidate. By contrast, only Protestants are included in the analysis of findings on the Catholic candidate, and only men in the analysis of findings on a woman candidate, since Catholics and women are sizable groups in the population and thus in the original samples.[35]

Prevalence of support for the value, as applied to blacks, Jews, and Catholics, increases substantially across the three major educational levels and remains undiminished even in the oldest age groups. Over the full range of education, the effects revealed by the gammas are always positive and, though modest, not insubstantial. The chi-squares, with occasional exceptions, are significant.[36]

It would be stretching the usual meaning of the term "minority" to apply it to the question about the nonconformist but well-qualified presidential candidate who was an "atheist." This 1959 finding, however, deserves inclusion because it enlarges upon the earlier evidence from the 1950s that the value of civil liberties was often denied to an atheist. In every age group and at every educational level, individuals were far less likely to support the candidacy of the atheist than that of conventional minority candidates. On the basis of the comparative findings, one might say that as recently as 1959 the atheist —as president—was truly anathema. And although the prevalence of support for him increased substantially across the three major educational levels, his candidacy seems too much for even most of the better educated of that period. The gammas are very low, and three out of four of the chi-square tests are not significant.[37]

The last item in table C.7.1 shows that the value of equality applied to the situation of a woman presidential candidate was already fairly prevalent throughout the male population in the late 1950s. In contrast with the atheist, a woman president was surely not anathema; but, in sharp contrast to all the other findings, the effects of education in this case were negligible. The gammas were as close to zero as they could get; the chi-squares in both cohorts were not significant, and although the prevalence increased between the least and most educated, the difference was relatively small. Surely, here is a flaw in the pattern of diffuse and general support by the educated of the value of political equality for minorities. We shall postpone discussion of the finding until we see how general it is in other periods. But before we pass over it, we should be reminded of what we have observed many times already. Any instrument measuring a value that is couched in a general fashion, or any that is formulated in terms of some single specification or application of that value, cannot do justice to the intricate patterning of such values over a variety of situations or provide comprehensive evidence on the effects of education.

Table C.7.2 presents evidence on the same four applications of the value of equality in the political sphere (excluding the case of the atheist), based on replicated findings in the early 1960s. With respect to the three minorities—blacks, Jews, and Catholics—for cohorts up to age sixty, the findings across the replications are very stable, positive, and highly consistent with the findings for the late 1950s. Among those over age sixty the replicated tests are consistent, the gammas showing diminished effects on two of the items and the chi-square tests suggesting no significant effects at all. Again we observe the strange flaw in the pattern of positive effects of education when the value is applied to the situation of a woman candidate, but we shall wait and see what happens in a later period before commenting.

Table C.7.3 presents replicated findings from two surveys in the late 1960s. When juxtaposed to table C.7.1, the later one provides evidence on generations separated by a full decade. For the three minorities—blacks, Jews, and Catholics—the findings, with minor exceptions, are stable across the two replications, are positive, and agree with the findings for earlier periods. Up to age sixty the effects of education are large, and over age sixty, although there is again some suggestion of a diminished effect, the effects are still substantial.[38] The consistent findings in the several periods, no matter which generation is involved or what kind of education and other formative experience it had, strongly suggest that education has positive and generalizable effects and that the slight diminution in the very oldest represents the inroads of aging. But surely the overall effects are large and long-enduring for the value as applied to blacks, Jews, and Catholics. Yet when the issue is support for a woman presidential candidate, the strange flaw in the pattern reappears in the late 1960s, taking the anomalous form in two of the tests of a *negative* sign and an inverse effect of education on this application of the value of equality. (The two negative gammas, however, are effectively zero in magnitude, as is a third gamma out of the four tests made.) Let us begin to unravel the mysterious flaw in the general pattern.[39]

The findings in these three time periods are based on five comparable surveys conducted by the Gallup Poll, the questions being identical in all the surveys. All five surveys were conducted outside an immediate campaign period, making the circumstances comparable. The *sequence* of the items we examined was basically the same,[40] the question about a woman candidate always being last, after the respondent had expressed himself on the three minority group candidates (whose respective locations in the sequence occasionally varied). But this only makes the incongruity in the pattern more surprising.[41] One would expect the respondents, and in turn the educational groupings, to feel some pressure to make their position on a woman candidate consistent with the stand they had already taken on the other three minorities—assuming they defined women as also a "minority." If they did not see women as exemplifying the general principle of equality for minorities but considered them a special and different case, then of course they would not feel they had contradicted themselves. Perhaps the finding implies that some unknown distinction was being made in the past that freed or diverted the better educated from applying their generally better values—not that the distinction deserves to be honored.

There is another possible explanation for the incongruity, subtle but simpler. For the three minorities, the question always referred to a "generally well-qualified man," who was then described as a member of the specified minority. But for reasons that defy understanding, the end clause in the question about a woman candidate was either "if she seemed qualified for the job" or "if she qualified for the job" or "if she were qualified for the job." The change in words and syntax may well have introduced real *doubt* or at least permitted the respondent to entertain doubt about competence. Indeed, it may be especially the highly educated, trained in the subtleties of syntax and sensitive to the conditional or subjunctive mode, in whose minds doubt has been raised. Thus freed from the imperative of acting on egalitarian principles, since a distinction in competence was implied, the appropriate conclusion is that the educated either quite properly withdraw their support or are given a rationale for acting upon whatever prejudices they might hold in this particular matter. This is as far as we can go in our attempts to understand the flaw in the pattern. As we shall see, the findings for the 1970s may add to the mystery, but, whatever its explanation, it is but one exception to a general pattern of large and enduring effects of education in expanding the realm in which the value of equality is applied.

Although they extend the temporal span of our conclusions, we hesitate to present findings from two NORC surveys in the 1970s, each of which included the pair of questions about a woman and a black presidential candidate. For one thing, the change in agency may obscure the influence of time and of the educational and other experiences of the particular newer generations studied. But, more important, the instrument has changed in ways that are subtle but, we now realize, important. The question on a woman candidate is now *first* rather than last in the sequence, the question on the black candidate coming forty or more questions later in the interview. Whereas the Gallup questions are imbedded in an irrelevant context of earlier questions, the prelude to the question on a woman candidate in both NORC surveys was two other questions on whether "women should take care of running their homes and leave running the country up to men," then a question on whether married women whose husbands are capable of supporting them should be engaged in gainful employment. This certainly heightens the salience of the traditional homemaker role of women and thus perhaps biases the findings on the woman candidate and makes them less comparable to the Gallup findings.[42]

Most important is the fact that both of the NORC questions described the candidate, then added the end clause "if she (he) were qualified for the job." NORC thereby remedied the defect in the Gallup battery, where the questions on women versus other minority candidates had differed in syntax. But it paid the price of casting a shadow of doubt over both candidates and making the wording of the NORC question on the black candidate no longer comparable to the Gallup question.

For all these reasons, we are uneasy about how to interpret the newest findings and how to evaluate any changes from the earlier findings. In the spirit of the value of freedom of information, the results are presented in table C.7.4. The replicated findings on the black candidate are highly unstable, sometimes showing large and significant effects, sometimes showing negligible and nonsignificant effects—clearly very different from the long run of consistent and large effects in all the earlier surveys. By the 1970s, even the lesser educated have moved closer to the ceiling, making it more difficult to register effects. The replicated findings on the woman candidate are somewhat unstable but tend, as in earlier periods, not to be significant.[43] We shall discount the new findings on a black candidate and conclude conservatively that education has positive, enduring, and pervasive effects on the value of equality of political opportunity, though there is one persistent flaw in the general pattern.

In table C.7.5, using only the comparable Gallup surveys and the two questions on the black and Jewish candidates—the only items for which the entire samples can be used—a series of cohort analyses are presented to provide further evidence on whether the positive effects of education endure with aging. In section A of the table, cohorts are aged by seven years; in section B by nine years, the oldest cohort in both instances advancing far into its sixties. On both items, there had been a trend across the nation in the 1960s toward greater support of candidates from these two minority groups; but, as in earlier cohort analyses, our interest is whether the various educational levels, all equally exposed to these common historical events, show any *differential* change as they age.

In section A the evidence shows unequivocally that there is no decline in the effects of education as cohorts advance into old age. In section B, there is no evidence of any decline of effect up to the point where individuals have reached their late fifties. In the cohort that has advanced up to age fifty-eight to sixty-nine, there is some suggestion of a decline of effect, but the evidence from our three statistical tests is mixed.

Weighing these many positive findings on how education affects the value of political equality applied to the support of well-qualified minority candidates, some readers may question the meaningfulness or validity of the findings. After all, about one-quarter of the population sampled in these surveys did not cast a vote for *anyone* in the elections of the period. Thus it might seem trivial, perhaps meaningless, to analyze whether they would vote for a hypothetical candidate from a minority group. Table C.7.6 thus repeats the earlier analyses but includes only those who reported that they had voted in the previous presidential election. As we noted in chapter 1, such self-reports have high validity. The issue is certainly meaningful for this group, and the triplicate evidence presented shows consistently that the effects of education are both good and large.[44]

Controls on Other Factors

The effects of education on the value of equality of opportunity applied to the situation of the three minorities—blacks, Jews, and Catholics—are not diminished by a series of controls. These tests, repeated on all the surveys before the 1970s, are highly consistent and are summarized in table D.4.[45] That the educational differences persist among southerners, especially on the item on a black presidential candidate, is compelling evidence that the effects are strong enough to survive in a hostile milieu.

Humane Values

Tables C.8.1–3, C.9, and C.10 present evidence on the effects of education in strengthening humane values. We looked for questions repeated in the surveys of several periods that would be indicators of humanitarianism—of support for practices designed to reduce pain, cruel punishment, deprivation, injury, violence, and suffering. We hoped that education's good works would go beyond inculcating support for the liberties of others, for their freedom from arbitrary constraints, for their equality of opportunity. That might still leave those others in a sorry state. If education also moved individuals toward the goals of reducing the suffering of others, that would be truly an impressive set of good works.

It was very difficult to find such a battery of questions, repeated over time, that measured a broad range of applications of humane values and that reasonable judges would agree were unambiguous measures of humanitarianism. The ambiguity stems not only from the limitations of the survey researchers who designed the questions but from deeper sources. Ironically, in real life desirable measures designed for humane purposes may also have undesirable consequences. Support for the measures we shall analyze—complex in their implications—may be judged by some to represent negative rather than positive effects of education, depending on which facet the judges examine. And the effects of education may turn out to be mixed and confusing, depending on the multiple facts—the pros and cons—that the more educated might perceive and balance in deciding their position.

Allowing Abortion

Tables C.8.1–3 present findings from a battery of questions dealing with the conditions under which abortion should be legally allowed, asked in the early and late 1960s and in the 1970s. The battery described a graded series of circumstances—never less than three but sometimes more—varying in the character and severity of the discomfort or suffering that would be alleviated by the abortion. Clearly, to support the legal right to an abortion for those individuals, *if they wish it*, is to favor reducing whatever burden has been described and to exhibit a humane value. But, just as clearly, in the eyes of some judges, the price paid for allowing that humane act is to condone killing. The latter act—at least in other circumstances—is far from humane. While we cannot resolve all ambiguity in interpreting the array of findings, it should be stressed that the questions *never* ask whether the respondent himself favors the abortion or would encourage others to have it, but only whether it should be legally allowed, if the other parties wish to avail themselves of it to reduce their burdens. And some of the questions describe burdens so severe that very little ambiguity can becloud those particular findings.

Items 1 and 2 in table C.8.1, used and replicated in surveys from the early 1960s and the 1970s, describe extreme situations where the "health of the mother is in danger" or the "child may be deformed." Abortions under these conditions clearly reduce great suffering and pain and possible death. Given such compelling reasons, to favor legalizing abortion seems close to an unambiguous expression of humane values. Indeed, as far back as the early 1960s, Americans saw little ambiguity in these situations. A very large majority supported the legalization of abortion in situation 1, except those over age sixty, among whom a smaller majority supported the measure. In situation 2 a somewhat smaller, but still substantial, majority supported the measure in the early 1960s. By the 1970s, close to 90% of all adults favored the measure in situation 1 and more than 80% favored it in situation 2, while only 3% remained undecided or conflicted.[46]

The most *recent* findings reveal that education has little or no effect in strengthening the humane values implicated in these two situations. Most of the tests are not significant. The gammas often are close to zero, though positive. Support is not substantially or consistently more prevalent among the more educated. Some might say everyone is so close to the ceiling by the 1970s, and the humane and merciful view of these situations now is so pervasive, that these two items are no longer sensitive indicators. But one cannot explain away the negative findings so easily. The findings on these items in the *earliest* period were also mixed, the effects of education being nonsignificant or negligible in magnitude in many of the tests. For the late 1960s the evidence is stronger, the gammas always positive and larger in magnitude and the prevalence of the values considerably greater among the more educated.

Taken all together, the effects of education on these two specific applications of the value surely are not impressive, albeit not totally negligible. Item 6, included in the battery in the 1970s, provides additional evidence. It describes a third extreme situation where the woman became pregnant as a result of rape. To alleviate the severe, involuntary burden such a mother must suffer also seems a relatively unambiguous criterion of humane values and was considered so by the public. In the aggregate, 80% endorsed the legalization of abortion in such circumstances and only 4% remained undecided. Although some of the chi-squares are not significant, the prevalence of the value as applied to this particular situation increases markedly with education on the replicated tests in all the cohorts, and the gammas are uniformly positive and substantial. Over these three extreme situations, the evidence in the 1970s is still mixed, but the general conclusion is not so tilted in a negative direction.

Item 3, asked in all the periods and replicated in the early 1960s and 1970s, describes the contrasted situation "where the family does not have enough money to support another child." An abortion would reduce deprivation and privation, and supporting its legalization can be construed as an expression of humane values. The circumstances, to be sure, are not as extreme as those described in items 1–2, and outside judges might be split, some regarding the item as an ambiguous criterion. Back in the 1960s, opposition generally prevailed. Although support had increased by the 1970s, those favoring the measure had become just a bare majority in the adult population.[47]

In the early 1960s, the replicated findings certainly provide no evidence that education strengthens the humane values implicated in situation 3 for any of the cohorts. Although most of the gammas are very close to zero, the negative signs may suggest the anomalous conclusion that the educated of that period were *less* sensitive to the plight of the poor family and to alleviating its burden through the avenue of legal abortion. Before advancing any hypothesis, let us look at the later findings. In the late 1960s, by contrast, the evidence is clear that in the two younger age-groups education has significant and substantial positive effects. Among individuals over age fifty, however, the effects are not significant and the gammas are considerably lower, although positive in sign. This pattern is not peculiar to those particular cohorts or generations and reappears in the replicated findings for the early 1970s. Once again, education has significant and substantial positive effects in the two younger age-groups (born about five years later than those measured in the late 1960s). Once again, among those over age fifty the effects are not significant and the gammas considerably lower, although positive in sign. Education has good and marked effects in heightening this application of humane values, but aging erodes some, if not all, of the effects.

Table C.8.2 summarizes the discrete findings for items 1–3, showing the average prevalence of support in each period, for each age-group or generation and the educational levels within it. The averages iron out the irregularities and present a clear, if gross, picture. Education has positive and enduring effects in this sphere of humane values, no matter which generations are examined. But one must not forget that this overall picture obscures the earlier confusing details: the modest or negligible effects on some discrete tests, the instability of the findings on replication, the occasional paradoxical patterns, the declines with aging on certain specific applications of the values, and the fact that all groups—young and old, more and less educated—sharply differentiate the circumstances in which they would apply humane values.

Some of the confusing detailed findings may be clarified, as before, by refined analyses. Table C.8.3 reexamines the effects of education on items 1–3 in all the time periods and replicated surveys, separately for Protestants and Catholics. Once again the separate analyses may reveal why the initial findings on the effects of education were often modest or negligible. If education in some periods had *intensified* the normal doctrinal position of Catholics, making them *less* supportive of the legal right to abortion in some or all of these circumstances, the combined findings would surely show modest effects and perhaps occasionally show the paradoxical form of an *inverse* effect of education. The refined analysis clearly and consistently shows sharply differential effects, positive and substantial among Protestants, modest or negligible or *inverse* among Catholics. The inverse effects (the negative signs) with one exception occur in the earlier historical periods, as one might expect. This analysis again circumscribes the effects of education in this sphere, limiting them mainly to those whose conception of humane values or the circumstances in which they should be applied was not guided by Catholic doctrines. For such individuals, the effects are far larger than one would have realized from the initial findings.[48]

Beginning in the late 1960s, item 4 was added to the battery. It anchors the other end of the scale and describes a situation with none of the dangers or deprivations included in items 1–3, one in which "the parents simply have all the children they want although there are no major health or financial problems involved in having another child."[49] However, support for a legal abortion under these circumstances does serve the humane goals of reducing the discomfort, dissatisfaction, and unhappiness an unwanted child brings and maximizing the freedom of choice of the family. Item 5, asked only in the 1970s, states that the "woman is not married and does not want to marry the man." On top of the burdens contained in situation 4 are the special burdens faced by an unwed mother and an "illegitimate" child.

No group—whether more or less educated, young or old—applies its values indiscriminately to these two special situations, support being far lower on these items than on items 1–3 and 6. But education does increase support. In the late 1960s, the effects on item 4 are substantial in the two younger age groups but decline in those over age fifty, the gammas being considerably lower and the differences nonsignificant. By the 1970s the national trend was toward increased support, but the differences between educational levels persist. Once again, the prevalence of the value increases with education. However, as before, the effects decline among those over age fifty. The findings are consistent in the replicated tests and in the two time periods. A similar pattern of effects is observed on item 5.[50]

So lengthy a battery of items in this sphere, so many tests within and across periods, so many comparisons among age-groups and generations, yield an extensive body of evidence. Understandably, the findings reveal occasional inconsistencies and may create some confusion. The weight of all the evidence, however, leads to the conclusion that education heightens humane values as applied to this special sphere; but often, though not always, the effects diminish after age fifty in the several generations examined. Some of the contrasted generations, to be sure, represent groups born only a few years apart, but other generations compared are separated by as much as a dozen years. There is the possibility that the pattern among the old and very old may be peculiar to a *set* of adjacent generations whose educational and other experiences were relatively similar, but there is enough evidence to entertain the hypothesis that the humane position in these matters, initially strengthened by education, is later undermined by aging.[51]

Controls on Other Factors

Table D.5 presents findings on the battery of questions on abortion when various social factors other than religion are controlled. The refined analysis by religion, already presented, establishes that the differences persist when the contrasted educational groups are matched in religion and all are Protestant.

Opposition to Capital Punishment

As we searched for indicators of humane values applied in other spheres, a question on approval or opposition to the death penalty for murder, asked repeatedly in surveys from the 1950s onward, seemed to us a relatively good criterion. The death penalty, in the phrase used by many learned judges, is *cruel and unusual* punishment, and to oppose it therefore seems a clear expression of humane values. Yet some regard such opposition as condoning or encouraging murder. Whatever ambiguity surrounds these findings, however, should be reduced when the findings from a second question are cited.

Over a long period there had been a nationwide trend toward increasing opposition to capital punishment; but in the late 1960s the demand for law and order and severe punishment for criminals produced a sharp reversal of the trend.[52] As noted in the earlier analyses, since all individuals and groups were exposed to the same atmosphere, any differential response of the contrasted educational groups can be observed.

Table C.9 shows with almost perfect uniformity that education has no effect whatsoever on this application of humane values. On item 1, in all the time periods, all the age-groups or generations involved, and all the replicated tests, the differences between educational groups are negligible and not significant, and the gammas are close to zero in magnitude. (A considerable number have a negative sign, but most of these are effectively zero.)

Some may say that the highly educated are being sensible, not inhumane, in favoring capital punishment as much as the lesser educated. Some might even argue that capital punishment deters violent crimes and therefore in the long run the position of the educated is humane. Subquestion 2, asked in variant ways in the early and late 1950s and the early 1960s, weakens this argument. Those who favored the death penalty for a convicted murderer were then asked whether a "teenager" or a "person under 21" should receive the death penalty for murder, special emphasis being given in one version to the possibility that he "should be spared because of his youth."[53] Here the humane view would be not to apply such cruel and irrevocable punishment to someone whose youthful actions might have been irresponsible and who might be corrigible. Yet here again, in three sets of tests based on item 2, the effects of education are found to be negligible. These findings reveal another persistent flaw in the pattern of effects of education on humane values.

Gun Control

A question on gun control asked over a long span of time and replicated in the 1970s provides a last measure of humane values. The question refers only to whether there should be a "law which would require a person to obtain a police permit before he or she could buy a gun." Thus it does not infringe the rights of responsible citizens to have guns for hunting or self-protection, but simply records or registers their ownership. By the screening process it insures in some degree that guns will not fall into the wrong hands and thereby serves the humane purposes of reducing violent injuries and deaths. Seemingly, the only ground on which a humane person would oppose it would be the belief that the procedure was totally ineffectual.

In answering the question, of course, all individuals may be responding to the temporary events of the period that would make the issue more or less dramatic as well as expressing their deeper values. But such stimuli are a constant and should not distort any differences between educational levels, and our findings from four surveys spanning fifteen years transcend particular events. In fact, over this long period, with minor exceptions most individuals —young or old, more or less educated—endorsed gun registration.

Table C.10 shows with almost complete uniformity that education has no effect on the humane values implicated in this situation for any of the age-groups or generations studied in the different time periods.[54] Another flaw in the pattern of effects in this sphere is revealed.

We have now completed our profile of the values of contrasted educational groups and examined whether the good features shaped by education deteriorate with age. We will summarize these findings and consider their implications in our conclusion.

3 Conclusion

Many measurements on thousands of adults aged twenty-five to seventy-two, drawn from thirty-eight national sample surveys conducted from 1949 to 1975 and thus representing the white students formerly taught in all the nation's schools and colleges over a long period, establish that education produces large and lasting good effects in the realm of values. The values of civil liberties not just for the orthodox but also for nonconformists, of due process of law, of freedom from the constraints of arbitrary laws in personal and social relations, of freedom for the flow of not only innocuous but also controversial information, of equality in the social, economic, and political spheres, and of humanitarianism or measures to reduce pain, injury, suffering, or deprivation, and also placing a higher valuation on morals or good conduct toward others than on manners, are more prevalent among adults who have gone to high school than among those who have not gone beyond elementary school. This profile of values is most prevalent among those who have gone to college.

The profiles within the various groups were similar whether the adults had their formal education and the other formative experiences of their childhood and later years in a relatively recent or distant era, and the groups appear sharply contrasted. The discrete values, the good features of the profile, often are 40% to 50% more prevalent among college graduates than among elementary-school graduates. And the gains from education are not reserved for those special groups who completed the full courses of instruction and graduated from high school or college. Small increments of education anywhere along the way from elementary school on into college were shown by several modes of analysis to have positive effects on values, although the contrast understandably is greatest when one compares the least and most educated groups. Despite aging, the contrasts persist. No matter which birth cohort or generation was examined, we found that the more educated preserved almost all their distinctive and attractive values up to age sixty. Beyond that stage of life, the differences on some values dwindle and occasionally disappear between ages sixty-one and seventy-two, but on many aspects the differences continue to be large. Even advanced aging cannot ravage the relatively attractive profile of the more educated.

We measured the specific application of a value to a series of concrete situations rather than the general endorsement of a good value in the abstract. Whether less or more educated, individuals did not apply their values indiscriminately. The nature of the situation affected their expression of a value and, in extreme instances, caused many to inhibit a value they usually exhibit. The educated, however, were far more likely to support the good value in situation after situation. Education does not shape a dull profile composed of lifeless features but works in some manner to make people more alert in seeing and active in supporting the good values implicated in a variety of concrete, often perplexing situations.

That the good values shaped by education are not only lively but *strong* was also established by various tests and measurements. Over the twenty-five years spanned by our surveys, the climate of opinion across the nation changed radically. Some of the measurements were obtained during times when the national climate was congenial to the values the educated exhibited. But it would hardly be fair to conclude that they manifested such values only when they were in fashion—when they were easy to express. Many of the measurements were obtained at points when those same good values were not in fashion. Whether the national climate was congenial or oppressive, even in the worst of times for libertarians and egalitarians, the educated were far more likely than the less educated to exhibit good values.

To take a particular stand when it meant, to put it poetically, to take arms against a sea of troubles was a demanding test of the strength of the values shaped by education. That the educated repeatedly exhibited particular values even when living in a local milieu whose norms were hostile provided additional compelling evidence of the strength of their values. And the many tests where the more educated supported certain values even though they ran counter to their own personal sympathies and beliefs were the final and compelling proof of the strength of those values.

No brief summary can cover all the detailed findings presented earlier. We have highlighted many of the good features of the profile of values formed by education rather than the minor blemishes and more serious flaws. It is not a perfect profile. But the flaws revealed under the penetrating light of hundreds of tests were few, observed mainly in complex situations where the privacy or humane value at stake either was ignored by the more educated or was overridden by other aspects of the situation.

The large, lasting, and diverse good effects on values found in this study, coupled with the very large, pervasive, and enduring effects in heightening knowledge, receptivity to knowledge, and information-seeking documented in our earlier study, establish that formal education has long been an important force throughout America in molding character as well as intellect. Our findings are bound to surprise the reader who has come to accept the continuing, widespread, and severe criticisms of educational institutions, and they therefore may raise skepticism rather than bring comfort. Better to turn some skepticism onto the critics.

As we remarked in our earlier study, "Much of such criticism is polemic and cannot be taken at face value. It is often based on meager evidence or none at all, or on empirical inquiries fraught with ambiguity" (p. 110). That some bad effects are, in fact, produced in some students from some institutions we have no doubt, but one must be careful not to exaggerate their magnitude or overgeneralize their extent. They surely provide no basis for impugning our findings on *enduring* effects among *nationwide* samples of adults from various periods, studied many years after they had completed their education. As we noted in 1975, evidence from educational research that is "generalizable to the nation for even *one* time point has been very rare. Evidence on the same scale for a series of points representing several cycles of operation of the educational system seems nonexistent, and evidence on the same scale about how long the effects endure into adult life is without doubt nonexistent" (p. 111). The review of the recent literature presented in the introduction to this book shows that the statement still applies.

Although we urge the reader not to reject our findings on the basis of the common criticisms and narrow studies in the literature, we are not suggesting that he accept our results uncritically. He should carefully weigh their generalizability in light of the many independent and well-designed samples drawn; their accuracy in light of the multiplicity of items used and the checks on biasing as well as random error of measurements; and the soundness of the conclusions in light of the multiple controls on the many factors that account for selective educational attainment and that might otherwise have contributed to spurious findings.[1]

The reader should also compare our findings with the few other secondary analyses that have drawn upon national surveys of the adult population to provide generalizable evidence about enduring effects of education in particular spheres. The studies by Withey and his associates and by Stember, both based on the pooling of massive data from various national surveys, do not use age and cohort breakdowns to trace how long the effects endure, but their overall findings on adults can be generalized and are consistent with our conclusions. The secondary analyses by Erskine and Siegel and by Hyman and Sheatsley, although smaller in scale, are national in scope and confirm our conclusions about civil liberties.[2] And primary analyses of particular national surveys sometimes include evidence on the effects of education that can be generalized to the nation, albeit limited to a single point in time and a narrow sphere of effects: Stouffer on civil liberties; Hyman and Sheatsley, and Campbell, on race relations; Almond and Verba on civic virtues; and Selznick and Steinberg on what they call the sphere of "enlightened culture," in which their analysis leads them to conclude that one "participates . . . only to the extent that one ascends the educational ladder"—these and other surveys all support our conclusion. Bowen also agrees with us in his careful review of published survey findings supplemented by some secondary analyses. He has concluded that education has enduring positive effects in diverse areas—moral development, practical affairs, citizenship, family relations, and leisure-time activities.[3]

Although we drew an elaborate profile composed of many features, our findings do not refute *all* the assertions that education is a weak or pernicious influence on values. The total realm of values is broad. The national surveys of good quality conducted between 1949 and 1975 did not explore every aspect of that broad realm, and we confined our own explorations to an even smaller region of values within which there would be little ambiguity and argument about these being *good* effects of education. Thus we do not have evidence to contradict all criticism. But this does not mean the critics are correct. As we have noted, thus far their sampling of populations has been too narrow, their study of cycles of the educational system too limited, and their coverage of the life span too truncated to support generalized criticism about the enduring effects of education.

For the time being, some of the specific questions about enduring effects will remain unanswered, but the research designs developed in our two studies, combined with the closely related strategy outlined in our earlier study, can soon lead toward the answers now lacking. Recent national surveys and "those that will accumulate in the future will produce a natural growth of questions . . . that could lead to further secondary analyses of the effects of education. Some of the items may simply replicate the present ones—all to the good . . . —but surely some of the new questions will enlarge the domain within which effects can be examined. No matter what special area . . . these items represent, the new data will soon bring us to the point where the effects of another cycle of education operating on a more recent cohort or generation can be examined."

However, as we noted then, "reliance on the *natural* growth of surveys will not yield enough data to strengthen secondary analyses [at] . . . the very points that most need to be buttressed. . . . A strategy of *semi*-secondary analysis is called for. The appropriate measures . . . can be piggybacked on future national surveys the agencies conduct, and these strategic services can be bought and paid for out of special funds" and, it should be added, at little cost. "The totality of future data, part created in the course of natural growth and part specially produced to suit the need, will provide the basis for more powerful semisecondary analyses of the enduring effects of education."[4]

The profile of values drawn in the present study, though not complete, seems to us attractive and elaborate enough to justify a confident conclusion about the good effects of education. Some critics, however, might accept the findings but still depreciate that conclusion. Out of zeal and from lofty aspirations, they might have developed such demanding standards for the schools that the effects we regard as large seem small to them. Given that vantage point, some are bound to look down on our findings. In setting reasonable standards, they must keep in mind the groups we have studied. These are not youths fresh out of school whose ideals have not yet been tested or tarnished. All are adults, some as much as fifty years away from the lessons they were taught. They may have learned some wisdom along the way, but they have also borne the endless burdens of ordinary living, and many have had to spend their lives in some narrow-minded circle. In the process, their better values may have fallen into neglect or become too costly to maintain. Traumatic events have afflicted some of them; prestigious and demagogic authorities have swayed others; institutions whose teaching is not as wholesome as that of the schools may have influenced them for long periods. Is it not surprising and heartening that they still show themselves to be as enlightened as we have found them?

Outlines of the Process Underlying the Effects

Our research did not attempt to describe the process underlying the effects of education. First things first. There is no point to explaining outcomes until one establishes that they have occurred. Our research was specially designed and was perhaps the unique avenue to establish the magnitude of enduring effects, and other kinds of research are now needed to trace in detail how the values are formed, solidified, modified, maintained, or eroded over the course of many years.[5] Nevertheless, careful examination of our procedures and findings does reveal some of the outlines of the processes that must be involved.

Once again, consider the measuring instruments. The questions posed an issue where the value was implicated in a concrete, often *contemporary*, case. For example, one of the questions in a 1954 survey described "a man whose loyalty has been questioned before a congressional committee, but who swears under oath he has never been a communist," and the respondent was then asked, "Should he be allowed to make a speech in your community?" The schools at the turn of the century might have taught some lessons on the eternal questions of liberty and perhaps have illustrated them with historical examples, but surely they could not have given specific instruction on this particular case. The McCarthy period involving such events was fifty years into the future. How then could it come about that those who had had more schooling so long ago were found to be more supportive of that man's civil liberties?

There was a parallel in our earlier study. Those with more education knew more academic and historical facts—for example, who Napoleon and Gutenberg were—but they also were found to be more informed about *current* events, which they could not possibly have learned while they were in school.

In the earlier study, the inference was inescapable that the effects of education came about not only through the implanting of specific knowledge but by increasing *receptivity* to new knowledge. The empirical evidence that more educated adults engaged in more information-seeking activities further clarified the process. A similar inference must be drawn here. Education may have taught the student some abstract moral principles and made him cherish some eternal values, but it also must have heightened his sensitivity to seeing the old values implicated in new situations and improved his capacities to think about complex issues involving values and to arrive at good decisions.

The outlines of the process are also revealed by our detailed findings. Elements *peculiar* to the formal schooling and informal educative experiences in any particular time period or locale cannot be *necessary* conditions for the good effects observed. Those effects transcended such boundaries in both the earlier and the current study. They occurred in the North and in the South, in individuals schooled before the turn of the century or recently, among men and women, and whether or not radio and television were present during the formative years of growth. However, once again the importance—but not the necessity—of one such set of conditions was revealed by the refined analyses summarized in tables D.1 to D.5. Among the more educated individuals who ended up at a station in life lower than is customary for the educated classes, effects were observed but were dampened. But less educated individuals who were fortunate enough to rise to higher stations in life than would be expected did not make up for their educational handicaps.

Our procedures and findings do not permit us to pinpoint the subtle aspects of the processes, but they do provide clues for those who continue the search to understand the good effects we have demonstrated.

The Relative Effects of Education on Knowledge and on Values

The findings in our two studies of the enduring effects of education are positive and show striking similarities in many respects. Yet, as one carefully inspects the two very long arrays of discrete findings, one is also struck by the difference between them. The good effects in the realm of values are diverse and are substantial in magnitude. But their cumulative weight in the mind's scales does not appear as great as that observed in the realm of knowledge. This weighing process cannot be utterly mechanical and, of course, can be deceptive. Noncomparability in the procedures used to obtain the two sets of findings could have led to a false conclusion about the relative effects, as could a switch in how they were weighed. But the two studies were designed to be comparable in essential respects, and uniform standards were applied to the findings. The effects of the same amounts of education obtained during the same historical cycles of the educational system by the same populations were examined in studying both realms, and the same statistical tests were applied to the results. To be sure, there were many more discrete tests of knowledge than there were of values, covering a wide and varied realm. It is a telling point that there were *fewer* negative findings. The effects pervaded every area of knowledge examined, and the pattern rarely departed from the monotonic —each increment of schooling usually produced a corresponding increase in knowledge. By contrast, blemishes and flaws in the profile of values, though not common, were noticeable, and departures from a monotonic pattern of effects were more frequent in this realm.

One other subtle problem arises in comparing the two sets of findings. If the items in the first study were very easy tests of knowledge, and the questions in the second study imposed severe strains on the person's good values, it seems logical that education would be bound to appear relatively more effective in increasing knowledge. Ideally, the measuring instruments should have been equal in difficulty. We were at the mercy of the questions in the available surveys, and we felt insecure about using any device to define and score equivalence in difficulty *across* two qualitatively different realms.[6] Fortunately, the items that happened to fall into the first study did not create such an obstacle in the present comparison of relative effects. Judging by the national norms the surveys automatically yield, most of the questions on knowledge were not very easy for ordinary adults to answer. Large majorities among the least-educated group failed many of the questions. The consistently positive findings of the first study occurred despite a series of difficult tests.

Relatively greater enduring effects on knowledge are to be expected on theoretical grounds. Analyze the relative difficulties facing the schools in increasing knowledge and in inculcating values, and the circumstances confronting the individual in later life that hinder or help the maintenance and growth of knowledge and values. A remark by a philosopher of education neatly states one difficulty in teaching values: "Since moral judgments are not statements of fact or pieces of information, they cannot be taught out of a text-book like the names of the capitals of European countries."[7] To be sure, books are not the only resources at the disposal of the school—not that one should minimize them—and the schools surely can rely to some extent on the teachers themselves to inculcate values. Here again, a difficulty that the distinguished educator George S. Counts sharply pointed out almost fifty years ago is still apropos of our discussion. "When the word indoctrination is coupled with education there is scarcely one among us possessing the hardihood to refuse to be horrified."[8] Counts may be regarded as a radical pamphleteer, and many would not follow his credo: "I am prepared to defend the thesis that all education contains a large element of imposition . . . that it is . . . eminently desirable, and that the frank acceptance of this fact by the educator is a major professional obligation."[9] But however horrified we may be by his position, we can nevertheless sense that his point is important for our analysis. Certainly, no one applies the word "indoctrination" when the schools try to teach most facts and *accepted* bodies of knowledge. That is regarded not as any unwarranted "imposition" but as a duty.

Those who teach know firsthand, and those who read the reports of educational testing programs know secondhand, that imparting knowledge is no simple task. But the schools and the teachers are equipped with all kinds of curricula, all sorts of materials, to make the learning easier and more palatable and are guided by some core of accepted principles proved in the long history of pedagogy and psychology. Contrast the circumstances for teaching and learning values. Here too there is a large relevant literature based in writings from moral philosophy, enlarged by works on moral and character education and psychological studies. But the teachers and schools, already faltering for fear of engaging in indoctrination, may be brought to a dead stop by the arguments, and the confusing and abstract tone, of much of that literature. The philosopher of education quoted earlier "gives us an important clue about method." What clue? "Children must learn to think about what it is like to be the other person. They must cultivate their sympathetic imaginations." How true. But where is the "important clue about method," and what comfort or guidance can the teacher take from his next remark? "This is not easy. It will not be brought about without effort on the part of parents and schoolmasters. And it will not be brought about by rational discussion alone."[10]

There is one more major difference between the two realms. In learning and maintaining knowledge in school and in later life, there are distractions, interruptions, even barriers, but there is little or no *opposition*. There are those who regard some body of knowledge as academic and useless and who think it is a waste of money to provide it. But those who oppose the pursuit of pure knowledge on the grounds that it is *bad* must surely be a tiny lunatic fringe. Consider the madman who argues that it is dangerous or wrong to learn that two and two make four. Indeed, there is much support for channeling more information to children and adults through many institutions. By contrast, there is strong opposition to the teaching or learning of almost any value, no matter how widely accepted, or to its application to a concrete case, from those who cherish the contrary value or implicate some other overriding value. Cremin, the distinguished historian of American education, recalls for us the "extraordinary influence of the nineteenth century common school . . . derived not so much from the common school per se as from a configuration of education of which the common school was only one element. Ordinarily including the white Protestant family, the white Protestant church, and the white Protestant Sunday school along with the common school, it was a configuration in which the *values* and pedagogies of the several component institutions happened to be mutually supportive."[11] In analyzing the present situation, although he remarks that "in some subject areas, of course, the school originates much of what it teaches," citing mathematics as an example, "in other realms . . . the domain of values and morals, the child has his first learning and possibly his most persuasive learning earlier and elsewhere. In these areas, it may be that the best the school can do is *engage* the instruction of the other educators and seek to strengthen or complement or correct or neutralize or countereducate."[12] Cremin stresses that other agencies, whose norms oppose those of the schools, are also socializing the child, but the same process extends throughout *adult* life, when other socializing agencies are also operative. The relative effects we observed fit Cremin's formulation: "It is not that schooling lacks potency: It is rather that the potency of schooling must be seen in relation to the potency of other experience."[13]

Given these challenging conditions, the enduring effects of education on values are all the more impressive.

Appendix A

Surveys and Questions Used
for Measurement of Values

Gallup Poll Surveys

443K—June 1949
Will you tell me what your understanding is of the term wiretapping?
1. *If any answer*: Do you think it is right (fair) or not to get evidence for use in a court trial by means of wiretapping?

443T—June 1949
Will you tell me what your understanding is of the term wiretapping?
1. *If any answer*: Do you approve or disapprove of allowing evidence which has been obtained by tapping private telephone wires to be used in a court trial?

445—July 1949
1. Some people say that, as long as the Communist Party is permitted by law in the United States, college and university teachers should be allowed to belong to the party and continue teaching. Do you agree or disagree?

452—January 1950
Will you tell me what your understanding is of the term wiretapping?
1. Identical to #1, 443T.

513—March 1953
1. Do you think former members of the Communist Party who have resigned from the party should or should not be allowed to teach in colleges and universities?

522—October 1953
1. Are you in favor of the death penalty for persons convicted of murder?
2. *If yes*: Are you in favor of the death penalty for persons under twenty-one who are convicted of murder?
3. Suppose a person known to favor communism wanted to make a speech in this city (town)—do you think he should be allowed to make the speech, or not?

Gallup Half of Stouffer Survey, May 1954

There are always some people whose ideas are considered bad or dangerous by other people.
For instance, somebody who is against all churches and religion.
1. If such a person wanted to make a speech in your city (town, community) against churches and religion, should he be allowed to speak, or not?
2. Should such a person be allowed to teach in a college or university, or not?
3. If some people in your community suggested that a book he wrote against churches and religion should be taken out of your library, would you favor removing this book, or not?

Or consider a person who favored government ownership of all the railroads and all big industries.

4. If this person wanted to make a speech in your community favoring government ownership of all the railroads and big industries, should he be allowed to speak, or not?

5. Should such a person be allowed to teach in a college or university, or not?

6. If some people in your community suggested that a book he wrote favoring government ownership should be taken out of your public library, would you favor removing the book, or not?

Now I should like to ask you some questions about a man who *admits he is a communist.*

7. Supposing he is teaching in a college. Should he be fired, or not?

8. Suppose this admitted communist wants to make a speech in your community. Should he be allowed to speak, or not?

9. Suppose he wrote a book which is in your public library. Somebody in your community suggests the book be removed from the library. Would you favor removing it, or not?

Now I would like you to think of another person. A man whose loyalty has been questioned before a congressional committee, but who swears under oath he has never been a communist.

10. Suppose he is teaching in a college or university. Should he be fired, or not?

11. Should he be allowed to make a speech in your community, or not?

12. Suppose he wrote a book which is in your public library. Somebody in your community suggests the book should be removed from the library. Would you favor removing it, or not?

588—August 1957

1. Are you in favor of the death penalty for persons convicted of murder? (Identical to #1, 522)

2. *If yes*: When a teenager commits a murder, and is found guilty by a jury, do you think he should get the death penalty or should he be spared because of his youth?

616—July 1959

1. Would you favor or oppose a law which would require a person to obtain a police permit before he or she could buy a gun?

621—December 1959

1. In some places in the United States it is not legal to supply birth control information. How do you feel about this? Do you think birth control information should be available to anyone who wants it, or not?

622—December 1959

1. Between now and 1960, there will be much discussion about the qualifications of presidential candidates—their education, age, religion, race, and the like. . . . If your party nominated a generally well-qualified man for president and he happened to be a Negro, would you vote for him?
2. If he happened to be a Jew?
3. If he happened to be a Catholic?
4. If he happened to be an atheist?
5. If your party nominated a woman for president, would you vote for her if she seemed qualified for the job?

662—August 1962

Do you think abortion operations should or should not be legal in the following cases:
1. Where the health of the mother is in danger?
2. Where the child may be born deformed?
3. Where the family does not have enough money to support another child?
4. Identical to #1, 621.

676—August 1963

1–4. There's always much discussion about the qualifications of presidential candidates—their education, age, race, religion, and the like. . . . Identical to #1–3, 5, 622.

702—November 1964

1. Identical to #1, 621

704—January 1965

1. Identical to #1, 616
2–3. Identical to #1, 2, 522.

705—January 1965

1. Some states have laws making it a crime for a white person and a Negro to marry. Do you approve or disapprove of such laws?

714—July 1965

Here are some questions on voting . . . do you think people who (cannot read or write English) should be permitted to vote, or not?
1. How about members of the Communist party?
2. How about members of the Ku Klux Klan? Do you think they should be permitted to vote, or not?
3. How about inmates of prisons?
4. How about atheists, that is, those who don't believe in God?
5–7. Identical to #1–3, 622.

721—December 1965

1–3. Identical to #1–3, 662

73

744—April 1967
1–4. Identical to #1–3, 5, 622

746—May 1967
1. Identical to #1, 522

776—March 1969
1–4. Identical to #1–3, 5, 622

785—July 1969
Do you happen to know what is meant by wiretapping? What are the arguments in favor of wiretapping? And what are the arguments against wiretapping?
1. Everything considered, would you say that, in general, you approve or disapprove of wiretapping?

788—September 1969
Do you think abortion operations should or should not be legal in the following cases:
1–3. Identical to #1–3, 662, followed by:
4. Where the parents simply have all the children they want although there are no major health or financial problems involved in having another child?

812—September 1970
Identical to #1, 705

846—February 1972
Identical to #1, 522

852—May 1972
Identical to #1, 616

934—August 1975
1. If your party nominated a woman for president, would you vote for her if she were qualified for the job?

NORC Surveys

351—January 1954
1. Do you think the Socialist party should be allowed to publish newspapers in this country?
2. Do you think members of the Communist party in this country should be allowed to speak on the radio?

NORC Half of Stouffer Survey, May 1954
Identical to #1–12, Gallup half of Stouffer survey.

404—April 1957
1 and 2, identical to #1–2, 351

(SRS) 330—December 1963

1. Do you think there should be laws against marriage between Negroes and whites?
2. Do you think Negroes should have the right to use the same parks, restaurants, and hotels as white people?
3. Do you think that Negroes should have as good a chance as white people to get any kind of job, or do you think that white people should have the first chance at any kind of job?

760—October 1964

1. Identical to #1, (SRS) 330

Suppose a man admitted in public that he did not believe in God:
2. Do you think he should be allowed to teach in a public high school?
3. Should he be allowed to hold public office?
4. Do you think that a book he wrote should be removed from a public library?

889A—June 1966

1. Identical to #3, (SRS) 330

4100—April 1970

1 & 2. Identical to #1–2, (SRS) 330

4119—March 1971

There are a lot of ways that people can try to influence what the government does. We are interested in knowing what you think of some of these ways.
1. If the government makes a decision that most people think is a good one, do you think other people should be allowed to criticize it—always, sometimes, or never?
2. Do you think people should be allowed to circulate petitions to ask the government to act on some issue—always, sometimes, or never?
3. Do you think people should be allowed to hold peaceful demonstrations to ask the government to act on some issue—always, sometimes, or never?
4. Do you think people should be allowed to block the entrance to a government building for a period of time to get the government to act on some issue that they think is important—always, sometimes, or never?
Now I'm going to read some statements. For each one, please tell me if you agree strongly, agree somewhat, disagree somewhat, or disagree strongly?
5. Police should be allowed to search meeting places of radical groups even though the police don't have a search warrant.
6. A person suspected of armed robbery should be kept in jail without bail to prevent him from committing any crime while he is waiting for his trial.
7. In order to protect itself, the government should be allowed to spy on anyone who is a member of a radical group even though that person may not have broken the law.

8. If someone is suspected of committing a crime the police should be allowed to search his home even though the police don't have a search warrant.

9. A radical who is suspected of inciting a riot should be kept in jail without bail to prevent him from committing any crime while he is waiting for his trial.

General Social Survey—Spring 1972

1. Identical to #1, Gallup 616
2. Do you favor or oppose the death penalty for persons convicted of murder?
3–11. Identical to #1–9 Stouffer 1954 Survey

General Social Survey—Spring 1973

1. Which *three* qualities listed on this card would you say are the most desirable for a child to have:

That he has good manners
That he tries hard to succeed
That he is honest
That he is neat and clean
That he has good sense and sound judgment
That he has self-control
That he acts like a boy (or she acts like a girl)
That he gets along well with other children
That he obeys his parents well
That he is responsible
That he is considerate of others
That he is interested in how and why things happen
That he is a good student

General Social Survey—Spring 1974

1. Identical to #1, Gallup 621
2–10. Identical to #1–9, Stouffer 1954 survey
11. Identical to #1, Gallup 616
12. Identical to #2, General Social Survey 1972

Please tell me whether or not you think it should be possible for a pregnant woman to obtain a *legal* abortion if:

13. If there is a strong chance of serious defect in the baby?
14. If she is married and does not want any more children?
15. If the woman's own health is seriously endangered by the pregnancy?
16. If the family has a very low income and cannot afford any more children?
17. If she became pregnant as a result of rape?
18. If she is not married and does not want to marry the man?
19. Everything considered, would you say that, in general, you approve or disapprove of wiretapping?
20. Do you think there should be laws against marriages between Negroes and whites?

21. If your party nominated a woman for president, would you vote for her if she were qualified for the job?

22. If your party nominated a Negro for president, would you vote for him if he were qualified for the job?

General Social Survey—Spring 1975

1. Identical to #1, Gallup 621
2. Identical to #1, NORC General Social Survey 1973
3–8. Identical to #13–18, NORC General Social Survey 1974
9. Identical to #19, NORC General Social Survey 1974
10. Identical to #20, NORC General Social Survey 1974
11. Identical to #21, NORC General Social Survey 1974
12. Identical to #22, NORC General Social Survey 1974
13. Identical to #1, Gallup 721
14. Identical to #1, NORC General Social Survey 1973

Appendix B

Tables on the Size and Shape of the Design
and Aggregate Size of Samples

Table B.1. Size and Shape of the Design for Studying
the Effects of Education on Values

A. Number of national surveys					B. Number of discrete tests of the general hypothesis			
Time Period	Gallup Poll	NORC	Total		Time Period	Gallup Poll	NORC	Total
1949–54	7[a]	2	9		1949–54	20[a]	14	34
1956–59	4	1	5		1956–59	9	2	11
1962–65	7	2	9		1962–65	23	6	29
1966–69	5	1	6		1966–69	14	1	15
1970–75	3	6	9		1970–75	3	59	62
Total over all time periods	26	12	38		Total over all time periods	69	82	151

[a]Gallup 443K and 443T, equivalent half-samples using two different forms of a question, were treated separately in our analysis and are therefore counted in the above tallies as two surveys and two tests. Similarly, the two equivalent surveys by Gallup and NORC that made up the Stouffer Inquiry into Civil Liberties were treated separately and are counted separately in the above tallies.

Table B.2. Aggregated Size of Samples for Various Estimates of the Effect of Education on Values

Time Period	Elementary School	College	Total Sample for Estimating Effects of All Levels of Education
Early 1950s			
Age 25–36	543	416	3,544
37–48	834	377	3,294
49–60	860	222	2,505
61–72	893	122	1,890
All ages	3,130	1,137	11,233
Late 1950s			
Age 25–36	137	200	1,586
37–48	254	154	1,607
49–60	342	117	1,337
61–72	368	71	1,126
All ages	1,101	542	5,656
Early 1960s			
Age 25–36	190	434	2,903
37–48	346	453	3,390
49–60	549	266	2,820
61–72	617	176	2,081
All ages	1,702	1,329	11,194
Late 1960s			
Age 25–36	84	356	1,929
37–48	163	279	1,967
49–60	267	175	1,548
61–72	254	106	1,174
All ages	768	916	6,618
Early 1970s			
Age 25–36	92	628	2,843
37–48	190	380	2,431
49–60	303	232	2,250
61–72	430	163	1,789
All ages	1,015	1,403	9,313
All time periods			
Age 25–36	1,046	2,034	12,805
37–48	1,787	1,643	12,689
49–60	2,321	1,012	10,460
61–72	2,562	638	8,060
Grand Total: All ages over all time periods	7,716	5,327	44,014

Note: Generally, only those with eight years of school were used to establish the maximum effects of elementary education. Some of the tests, because of the cruder codes, included individuals with fewer than eight years. The aggregated size of the elementary-school samples include these. In three surveys, because of the codes, groupings defining the four stages of aging depart slightly from the categories shown, and the numbers involved are included in the aggregated size of samples at the four age stages.

Appendix C

Tables of Basic Findings

Table C.1. The Effects of Education on the Hierarchy of Values
Considered Desirable for Children in the Early 1970s

Value	Percentage Ranking the Value as One of Three Most Important			Relationship over Full Range of Variables	
	Elementary School	High School	College	p	γ
1. Being considerate of others					
Age 25–36 1973 survey	25 (12)[a]	33 (131)	51 (72)	*[b]	.30
1975 survey	29 (7)	27 (127)	46 (81)	**	.34
Age 37–48 1973 survey	5 (19)	36 (88)	47 (53)	**	.33
1975 survey	36 (11)	32 (100)	58 (48)	**	.32
Age 49–60 1973 survey	16 (25)	28 (90)	32 (22)	*	.18
1975 survey	26 (27)	30 (89)	38 (24)	ns	.28
Age 61–72 1973 survey	7 (43)	24 (46)	60 (15)	**	.37
1975 survey	3 (35)	31 (45)	13 (16)	**	.26
2. Being responsible					
Age 25–36 1973 survey	25 (12)	36 (131)	44 (72)	**	.24
1975 survey	14 (7)	37 (127)	53 (81)	*	.21
Age 37–48 1973 survey	37 (19)	32 (88)	49 (53)	*	.23
1975 survey	18 (11)	44 (100)	46 (48)	*	.16
Age 49–60 1973 survey	24 (25)	37 (90)	36 (22)	*	.24
1975 survey	33 (27)	33 (89)	58 (24)	*	.34
Age 61–72 1973 survey	12 (43)	30 (46)	33 (15)	ns	.17
1975 survey	17 (35)	27 (45)	50 (16)	**	.39
3. Having good sense and sound judgment					
Age 25–36 1973 survey	25 (12)	38 (131)	35 (72)	ns	.06
1975 survey	0 (7)	43 (127)	52 (81)	*	.21
Age 37–48 1973 survey	21 (19)	47 (88)	53 (53)	ns	.20
1975 survey	27 (11)	43 (100)	54 (48)	ns	.20
Age 49–60 1973 survey	20 (25)	42 (90)	64 (22)	ns	.22
1975 survey	30 (27)	28 (89)	46 (24)	ns	.15
Age 61–72 1973 survey	23 (43)	39 (46)	33 (15)	ns	.12
1975 survey	29 (35)	16 (45)	38 (16)	ns	.07
4. Being interested in how and why things happen					
Age 25–36 1973 survey	17 (12)	21 (131)	36 (72)	ns	.16
1975 survey	14 (7)	13 (127)	20 (81)	*	.25
Age 37–48 1973 survey	16 (19)	26 (88)	32 (53)	ns	.23
1975 survey	18 (11)	11 (100)	21 (48)	**	.21
Age 49–60 1973 survey	12 (25)	19 (90)	18 (22)	ns	.22
1975 survey	4 (27)	12 (89)	21 (24)	ns	.15
Age 61–72 1973 survey	12 (43)	17 (46)	27 (15)	ns	.19
1975 survey	6 (35)	11 (45)	13 (16)	*	—.03

Note: NORC General Social Surveys, spring 1973 and 1975. Elementary school equals grade 8. In this and following tables, the high school and college groups include graduates only.

[a]In this and following tables, N (number in sample) follows percentage (in parentheses).

[b]In this and following tables, probabilities are stated as follows: $* = p \leq .05$; $** = p \leq .01$; $*** = p \leq .001$; ns = not significant.

Table C.1. (Cont.)

Value	Percentage Ranking the Value as One of Three Most Important			Relationship over Full Range of Variables	
	Elementary School	High School	College	p	γ
5. Being honest					
Age 25–36 1973 survey	67 (12)	73 (131)	68 (72)	***	.12
1975 survey	86 (7)	79 (127)	64 (81)	ns	—.17
Age 37–48 1973 survey	47 (19)	71 (88)	40 (53)	***	—.20
1975 survey	82 (11)	84 (100)	63 (48)	*	—.21
Age 49–60 1973 survey	72 (25)	70 (90)	55 (22)	ns	.04
1975 survey	74 (27)	76 (89)	67 (24)	ns	—.07
Age 61–72 1973 survey	56 (43)	76 (46)	47 (15)	*	—.03
1975 survey	77 (35)	67 (45)	63 (16)	ns	—.11
6. Being neat and clean					
Age 25–36 1973 survey	17 (12)	6 (131)	1 (72)	ns	—.24
1975 survey	14 (7)	6 (127)	3 (81)	*	—.30
Age 37–48 1973 survey	26 (19)	5 (88)	0 (53)	**	—.29
1975 survey	0 (11)	4 (100)	2 (48)	ns	—.11
Age 49–60 1973 survey	20 (25)	8 (90)	0 (22)	*	—.24
1975 survey	7 (27)	8 (89)	0 (24)	ns	—.17
Age 61–72 1973 survey	21 (43)	7 (46)	13 (15)	ns	—.09
1975 survey	14 (35)	9 (45)	6 (16)	ns	—.12
7. Having good manners					
Age 25–36 1973 survey	50 (12)	24 (131)	6 (72)	***	—.31
1975 survey	29 (7)	20 (127)	10 (81)	ns	—.19
Age 37–48 1973 survey	37 (19)	10 (88)	11 (53)	*	—.17
1975 survey	27 (11)	15 (100)	4 (48)	***	—.22
Age 49–60 1973 survey	32 (25)	21 (90)	5 (22)	ns	—.20
1975 survey	37 (27)	21 (89)	13 (24)	***	—.21
Age 61–72 1973 survey	37 (43)	15 (46)	0 (15)	ns	—.20
1975 survey	37 (35)	31 (45)	6 (16)	ns	—.13

Table C.2.1. The Effects of Education on the Values of Civil Liberties for Nonconformists in the Early 1950s

Civil Liberty	Percentage Supporting Liberty			Relationship over Full Range of Variables	
	Elementary School	High School	College	p	γ
1. *Allow speech against religion*[a]					
Age 30–39	24 (121)	50 (183)	77 (60)	***	.45
40–49	19 (171)	38 (119)	67 (45)	***	.43
50–59	22 (180)	38 (55)	52 (23)	***	.37
60 or over	19 (305)	36 (64)	46 (13)	*	.24
2. *Allow book against religion in public library*[a]					
Age 30–39	19 (121)	47 (183)	78 (60)	***	.47
40–49	20 (171)	45 (119)	67 (45)	***	.42
50–59	26 (180)	35 (55)	39 (23)	ns	.22
60 or over	18 (305)	33 (64)	46 (13)	**	.06
3. *Allow antagonist of religion to teach in a college*[a]					
Age 30–39	3 (121)	13 (183)	45 (60)	***	.48
40–49	6 (171)	15 (119)	31 (45)	***	.37
50–59	6 (180)	11 (55)	4 (23)	ns	.09
60 or over	9 (305)	3 (64)	15 (13)	ns	—.35
4. *Allow speech for government ownership*[a]					
Age 30–39	50 (121)	65 (183)	97 (60)	***	.36
40–49	48 (171)	69 (119)	80 (45)	***	.28
50–59	46 (180)	64 (55)	74 (23)	**	.31
60 or over	43 (305)	63 (64)	77 (13)	**	.17
5. *Allow book for government ownership in public library*[a]					
Age 30–39	40 (121)	61 (183)	82 (60)	***	.31
40–49	40 (171)	62 (119)	73 (45)	***	.28
50–59	49 (180)	55 (55)	65 (23)	ns	.11
60 or over	35 (305)	58 (64)	69 (13)	***	.16
6. *Allow proponent of government ownership to teach in a college*[a]					
Age 30–39	31 (121)	36 (183)	53 (60)	**	.08
40–49	27 (171)	35 (119)	47 (45)	*	.12
50–59	29 (180)	31 (55)	30 (23)	ns	.04
60 or over	28 (305)	19 (64)	39 (13)	**	—.22

[a]Stouffer study, NORC 1954 survey; elementary school equals grades 1–8.

Table C.2.1. (Cont.)

Civil Liberty	Percentage Supporting Liberty			Relationship over Full Range of Variables	
	Elementary School	High School	College	p	γ
7. *Allow admitted communist to make speech*[a]					
Age 30–39	17 (121)	26 (183)	68 (60)	***	.39
40–49	16 (171)	26 (119)	51 (45)	***	.34
50–59	21 (180)	27 (55)	48 (23)	ns	.27
60 or over	16 (305)	25 (64)	23 (13)	ns	.14
8. *Allow book by admitted communist in public library*[a]					
Age 30–39	12 (121)	32 (183)	73 (60)	***	.47
40–49	12 (171)	36 (119)	62 (45)	***	.43
50–59	14 (180)	27 (55)	35 (23)	***	.33
60 or over	13 (305)	22 (64)	39 (13)	ns	.13
9. *Allow admitted communist to teach in a college*[a]					
Age 30–39	7 (121)	7 (183)	17 (60)	**	.11
40–49	5 (171)	7 (119)	11 (45)	ns	.16
50–59	3 (180)	6 (55)	9 (23)	ns	.07
60 or over	3 (305)	11 (64)	23 (13)	**	.12
Mean percentage (items 1–9)					
Age 30–39	23	37	66		
40–49	21	37	54		
50–59	24	33	40		
60 or over	20	30	42		
10. *Allow suspected communist to make speech*[a]					
Age 30–39	61 (121)	75 (183)	83 (60)	**	.28
40–49	63 (171)	83 (119)	80 (45)	*	.27
50–59	66 (180)	60 (55)	78 (23)	**	.14
60 or over	60 (305)	75 (64)	85 (13)	ns	.27
11. *Allow book by suspected communist in public library*[a]					
Age 30–39	60 (121)	78 (183)	92 (60)	***	.33
40–49	67 (171)	80 (119)	84 (45)	*	.25
50–59	62 (180)	58 (55)	78 (23)	*	.15
60 or over	60 (305)	67 (64)	85 (13)	ns	.15

Table C.2.1. (Cont).

	Percentage Supporting Liberty			Relationship over Full Range of Variables	
Civil Liberty	Elementary School	High School	College	p	γ
12. *Allow suspected communist to teach in a college*[a]					
Age 30–39	62 (121)	71 (183)	85 (60)	**	.21
40–49	64 (171)	81 (119)	80 (45)	*	.23
50–59	64 (180)	64 (55)	78 (23)	**	.20
60 or over	61 (305)	59 (64)	85 (13)	ns	.01

	10–12	*7–9*	*10–12*	*7–9*	*10–12*	*7–9*
Mean percentage						
Age 30–39	61	12	75	22	87	53
40–49	65	11	81	23	81	38
50–59	64	13	61	20	78	31
60 or over	60	11	67	19	85	28

	Percentage Supporting Liberty			Relationship over Full Range of Variables	
Civil Liberty	Elementary School	High School	College	p	γ
13. *Allow advocate of communism to make speech*[b]					
Age 25–36	31 (35)	32 (162)	70 (43)	***	.36
37–48	21 (91)	32 (113)	59 (34)	***	.32
49–60	13 (77)	29 (49)	37 (19)	**	.40
61–72	21 (58)	17 (18)	39 (13)	ns	.03
14. *Allow former communist to teach in a college*[c]					
Age 25–36	18 (61)	24 (161)	67 (39)	***	.29
37–48	14 (85)	25 (94)	35 (23)	ns	.19
49–60	19 (102)	17 (64)	29 (14)	ns	.08
61–72	15 (55)	10 (20)	31 (13)	ns	—.06
15. *Allow member of communist party to teach in a college*[d]					
Age 25–36	13 (87)	18 (193)	20 (70)	**	.05
37–48	14 (131)	15 (153)	27 (71)	***	.04
49–60	7 (139)	6 (96)	12 (49)	*	—.18
61–72	8 (76)	3 (39)	16 (19)	ns	—.14
Mean percentage (items 13–15)					
Age 25–36	21	25	52		
37–48	16	24	40		
49–60	13	17	26		
61–72	15	10	29		

[b]Gallup 522—October 1953; elementary school equals grades 7–8.
[c]Gallup 513—March 1953; elementary school equals grades 7–8.
[d]Gallup 445—July 1949; elementary school equals grades 7–8.

Table C.2.1. (Cont).

Civil Liberty	Percentage Supporting Liberty			Relationship over Full Range of Variables	
	Elementary School	High School	College	p	γ
16. *Allow Socialist party to publish newspapers*[e, f]					
Age 25–34 1954 survey	31 (29)	42 (71)	86 (28)	**	.38
1957 survey	13 (30)	48 (109)	77 (35)	***	.41
35–44 1954 survey	30 (33)	50 (54)	80 (20)	***	.32
1957 survey	28 (39)	44 (86)	84 (19)	***	.35
45–54 1954 survey	34 (35)	46 (26)	75 (12)	**	.33
1957 survey	19 (58)	51 (49)	76 (21)	***	.40
55–64 1954 survey	45 (20)	46 (11)	71 (7)	*	.38
1957 survey	29 (101)	58 (33)	86 (21)	***	.37
17. *Allow member of communist party to speak on radio*[e, f]					
Age 25–34 1954 survey	14 (29)	20 (71)	25 (28)	***	.34
1957 survey	3 (30)	18 (109)	37 (35)	***	.50
35–44 1954 survey	21 (33)	17 (54)	15 (20)	ns	.12
1957 survey	10 (39)	8 (86)	47 (19)	***	.32
45–54 1954 survey	9 (35)	15 (26)	25 (12)	**	.26
1957 survey	7 (58)	27 (49)	43 (21)	**	.39
55–64 1954 survey	15 (20)	9 (11)	0 (7)	ns	—.07
1957 survey	8 (101)	15 (33)	29 (21)	***	.31

[e]NORC 351—January 1954; elementary school equals grades 7–8.
[f]NORC 404—April 1957; elementary school equals grades 7–8.

Table C.2.2. The Effects of Education on the Values of Civil Liberties for Nonconformists in the Early 1960s

Civil Liberty	Percentage Supporting Liberty			Relationship over Full Range of Variables	
	Elementary School	High School	College	p	γ
A. Liberty for Nonconformist and Freedom of Information					
1. *Allow book by admitted atheist in public library*[a]					
Age 25–36	38 (8)	81 (98)	92 (25)	**	.42
37–48	43 (28)	74 (169)	91 (79)	***	.48
49–60	51 (35)	71 (163)	91 (42)	***	.42
61–72	44 (52)	73 (67)	71 (21)	**	.32
2. *Allow admitted atheist to teach in public high school*[a]					
Age 25–36	38 (8)	54 (98)	76 (25)	*	.38
37–48	32 (28)	43 (170)	66 (79)	**	.32
49–60	39 (36)	44 (164)	60 (42)	ns	.23
61–72	25 (53)	43 (67)	64 (22)	ns	.23
B. Liberty for Nonconformist					
3. *Allow admitted atheist to hold public office*[a]					
Age 25–36	0 (8)	52 (98)	75 (25)	**	.43
37–48	50 (28)	43 (169)	72 (79)	***	.33
49–60	50 (36)	44 (164)	69 (42)	*	.19
61–72	34 (53)	51 (67)	68 (22)	**	.29
4. *Allow atheist to vote*[b]					
Age 25–36	38 (16)	76 (128)	92 (37)	***	.56
37–48	39 (26)	77 (141)	89 (35)	***	.47
49–60	54 (56)	83 (71)	92 (26)	***	.52
61–72	55 (44)	76 (21)	74 (19)	**	.41
5. *Allow member of communist party to vote*[b]					
Age 25–36	0 (16)	20 (128)	46 (37)	**	.28
37–48	4 (26)	23 (141)	46 (35)	***	.32
49–60	16 (56)	25 (71)	50 (26)	***	.24
61–72	11 (44)	24 (21)	21 (19)	ns	.17

[a]NORC 760—October 1964; elementary school equals grade 8.
[b]Gallup 714—July 1965; elementary school equals grade 8.

Table C.2.2. (Cont.)

Civil Liberty	Percentage Supporting Liberty			Relationship over Full Range of Variables	
	Elementary School	High School	College	p	γ
6. *Allow member of Ku Klux Klan to vote*[b]					
Age 25–36	31 (16)	55 (128)	73 (37)	ns	.21
37–48	27 (26)	50 (141)	80 (35)	**	.17
49–60	30 (56)	49 (71)	89 (26)	***	.25
61–72	43 (44)	52 (21)	68 (19)	ns	.03
7. *Allow prison inmates to vote*[b]					
Age 25–36	38 (16)	40 (128)	41 (37)	ns	—.11
37–48	39 (26)	34 (141)	26 (35)	***	—.24
49–60	45 (56)	35 (71)	31 (26)	***	—.13
61–72	30 (44)	33 (21)	16 (19)	ns	—.10
Mean percentage (items 1–4)					
Age 25–36	29	66	84		
37–48	41	59	80		
49–60	49	61	78		
61–72	40	61	69		
Mean percentage (items 5–7)					
Age 25–36	23	50	70		
37–48	23	50	72		
49–60	33	52	77		
61–72	36	51	54		

Table C.2.3. The Effects of Education on the Values of Civil Liberties for Nonconformists in the Early 1970s

Civil Liberty	Percentage Supporting Liberty			Relationship over Full Range of Variables	
	Elementary School	High School	College	p	γ
A. Liberty for Nonconformist and Freedom of Information					
1. Allow speech against religion					
Age 25–36 1972 survey[a]	57 (7)	81 (126)	96 (78)	***	.57
1974 survey[b]	44 (9)	70 (128)	94 (82)	***	.62
Age 37–48 1972 survey	48 (21)	77 (102)	94 (34)	***	.45
1974 survey	50 (18)	73 (112)	94 (47)	***	.52
Age 49–60 1972 survey	24 (38)	67 (90)	86 (29)	***	.51
1974 survey	36 (31)	58 (81)	73 (30)	**	.36
Age 61–72 1972 survey	36 (31)	53 (38)	90 (19)	***	.33
1974 survey	28 (36)	49 (35)	64 (25)	**	.45
2. Allow book against religion in public library					
Age 25–36 1972 survey	57 (7)	74 (126)	94 (78)	***	.53
1974 survey	33 (9)	66 (128)	89 (82)	***	.52
Age 37–48 1972 survey	43 (21)	74 (102)	94 (34)	***	.46
1974 survey	61 (18)	64 (112)	98 (47)	***	.47
Age 49–60 1972 survey	21 (38)	64 (90)	90 (29)	***	.48
1974 survey	42 (31)	49 (81)	77 (30)	***	.37
Age 61–72 1972 survey	26 (31)	50 (38)	84 (19)	***	.42
1974 survey	22 (36)	51 (35)	64 (25)	**	.36
3. Allow antagonist of religion to teach in a college					
Age 25–36 1972 survey	29 (7)	52 (126)	85 (78)	***	.50
1974 survey	33 (9)	47 (128)	76 (82)	**	.39
Age 37–48 1972 survey	33 (21)	42 (102)	61 (33)	**	.21
1974 survey	28 (18)	38 (112)	64 (47)	**	.37
Age 49–60 1972 survey	8 (38)	22 (90)	62 (29)	***	.28
1974 survey	19 (31)	25 (81)	67 (30)	**	.37
Age 61–72 1972 survey	10 (31)	32 (38)	56 (18)	***	.16
1974 survey	6 (36)	20 (35)	28 (25)	ns	.31

[a]NORC General Social Survey—March 1972; elementary school equals grade 8.
[b]NORC General Social Survey—March 1974; elementary school equals grade 8.

Table C.2.3. (Cont.)

Civil Liberty	Percentage Supporting Liberty			Relationship over Full Range of Variables	
	Elementary School	High School	College	p	γ
4. *Allow speech for government ownership*					
Age 25–36 1972 survey	71 (7)	88 (126)	97 (78)	**	.49
1974 survey	89 (9)	81 (128)	96 (82)	**	.45
Age 37–48 1972 survey	76 (21)	89 (102)	94 (34)	***	.49
1974 survey	72 (18)	80 (112)	96 (47)	*	.33
Age 49–60 1972 survey	47 (38)	80 (90)	93 (29)	***	.40
1974 survey	55 (31)	72 (81)	90 (30)	*	.28
Age 61–72 1972 survey	58 (31)	74 (38)	100 (19)	**	.31
1974 survey	44 (36)	74 (35)	76 (25)	ns	.29
5. *Allow book for government ownership in public library*					
Age 25–36 1972 survey	57 (7)	74 (126)	92 (78)	***	.40
1974 survey	44 (9)	77 (127)	94 (82)	***	.50
Age 37–48 1972 survey	65 (20)	76 (102)	94 (34)	***	.44
1974 survey	61 (18)	71 (111)	98 (47)	**	.40
Age 49–60 1972 survey	42 (38)	75 (89)	86 (29)	***	.40
1974 survey	45 (31)	70 (81)	90 (30)	***	.34
Age 61–72 1972 survey	45 (31)	61 (38)	95 (19)	***	.36
1974 survey	36 (36)	71 (35)	60 (25)	ns	.28
6. *Allow proponent of government ownership to teach in a college*					
Age 25–36 1972 survey	57 (7)	64 (126)	90 (78)	***	.41
1974 survey	78 (9)	65 (127)	88 (82)	*	.33
Age 37–48 1972 survey	48 (21)	61 (102)	76 (33)	***	.31
1974 survey	39 (18)	52 (111)	70 (47)	*	.23
Age 49–60 1972 survey	42 (38)	40 (90)	59 (29)	**	.04
1974 survey	32 (31)	44 (81)	80 (30)	*	.26
Age 61–72 1972 survey	42 (31)	34 (38)	74 (19)	***	.08
1974 survey	28 (36)	40 (35)	36 (25)	ns	.01
7. *Allow admitted communist to make speech*					
Age 25–36 1972 survey	29 (7)	51 (125)	91 (78)	***	.56
1974 survey	33 (9)	64 (128)	92 (82)	***	.54
Age 37–48 1972 survey	29 (21)	55 (102)	94 (34)	***	.53
1974 survey	61 (18)	63 (112)	89 (47)	***	.50
Age 49–60 1972 survey	18 (38)	50 (90)	86 (29)	***	.49
1974 survey	36 (31)	56 (79)	73 (30)	**	.36
Age 61–72 1972 survey	19 (31)	47 (38)	58 (19)	**	.43
1974 survey	31 (36)	51 (35)	44 (25)	ns	.24

Table C.2.3. (Cont.)

Civil Liberty	Percentage Supporting Liberty			Relationship over Full Range of Variables	
	Elementary School	High School	College	p	γ
8. *Allow book by admitted communist in public library*					
Age 25–36 1972 survey	14 (7)	61 (124)	87 (78)	***	.51
1974 survey	44 (9)	65 (127)	90 (82)	***	.53
Age 37–48 1972 survey	38 (21)	63 (102)	91 (34)	***	.47
1974 survey	61 (18)	63 (111)	94 (47)	***	.47
Age 49–69 1972 survey	22 (37)	50 (90)	82 (28)	***	.45
1974 survey	23 (31)	50 (80)	80 (30)	***	.41
Age 61–72 1972 survey	13 (31)	45 (38)	84 (19)	***	.55
1974 survey	31 (36)	51 (35)	56 (25)	ns	.28
9. *Allow admitted communist to teach in a college*					
Age 25–36 1972 survey	14 (7)	35 (125)	65 (77)	***	.45
1974 survey	22 (9)	44 (127)	77 (82)	***	.42
Age 37–48 1972 survey	19 (21)	33 (102)	50 (34)	*	.22
1974 survey	33 (18)	26 (112)	62 (47)	***	.34
Age 49–60 1972 survey	13 (38)	20 (90)	43 (28)	*	.17
1974 survey	26 (31)	24 (79)	50 (30)	ns	.25
Age 61–72 1972 survey	13 (31)	18 (38)	35 (17)	ns	.25
1974 survey	19 (36)	23 (35)	44 (25)	ns	.15
Mean percentage (items 1–9)					
Age 25–36	45	64	89		
37–48	48	62	84		
49–60	31	51	76		
61–72	28	47	64		

B. Liberty for Nonconformist

	Percentage Supporting Liberty			Relationship over Full Range of Variables	
10. *Strongly oppose right of police to search radical meeting places without warrant*c					
Age 25–36	0 (13)	12 (113)	41 (64)	***	.32
37–48	8 (24)	16 (103)	48 (40)	***	.20
49–60	8 (25)	9 (68)	41 (22)	*	.29
61–72	9 (55)	23 (43)	13 (16)	ns	.08

Table C.2.3. (Cont.)

Civil Liberty	Percentage Supporting Liberty			Relationship over Full Range of Variables	
	Elementary School	High School	College	p	γ
11. *Strongly oppose jailing without bail radical suspected of inciting riot*[c]					
Age 25–36	8 (13)	5 (114)	41 (64)	***	.30
37–48	13 (23)	9 (103)	48 (40)	***	.33
49–60	0 (25)	10 (67)	41 (22)	***	.42
61–72	2 (54)	11 (44)	18 (17)	*	.24
12. *Strongly oppose right of government to spy on members of radical groups*[c]					
Age 25–36	8 (13)	25 (110)	44 (64)	*	.27
37–48	21 (24)	17 (103)	58 (40)	***	.31
49–60	8 (26)	18 (67)	41 (22)	*	.23
61–72	7 (55)	17 (42)	11 (18)	ns	.18
Mean percentage (items 10–12)					
Age 25–36	5	14	42		
37–48	14	14	51		
49–60	5	12	41		
61–72	6	17	14		
13. *Strongly oppose right of police to search home of criminal suspect without warrant*[c]					
Age 25–36	31 (13)	30 (113)	56 (64)	*	.20
37–48	38 (24)	33 (104)	68 (40)	*	.11
49–60	12 (26)	35 (69)	55 (22)	*	.33
61–72	11 (54)	39 (44)	44 (18)	ns	.14
14. *Strongly oppose jailing without bail suspect in armed robbery*[c]					
Age 25–36	0 (13)	11 (114)	28 (64)	*	.22
37–48	4 (24)	5 (103)	30 (40)	***	.27
49–60	4 (25)	12 (69)	29 (21)	ns	.15
61–72	4 (55)	11 (44)	17 (18)	ns	.18

[c]NORC 4119—March 1971; elementary school equals grade 8.

Table C.2.4. The Effects of Education on the Values of Civil Liberties in Independent Simultaneous Surveys in 1954

Civil Liberty	Increase in Prevalence among College Graduates Contrasted with Elementary School Educated	
	NORC	*Gallup Poll*
Allow speech against religion		
Age 30–39	53%	39%
40–49	48	55
50–59	30	32
60 or over	27	25
Gamma over full range of education, all ages combined	.43	.41
Allow book against religion in public library		
Age 30–39	59%	50%
40–49	47	48
50–59	13	40
60 or over	28	—1
Gamma over full range of education, all ages combined	.38	.38
Allow antagonist of religion to teach in a college		
Age 30–39	42%	29%
40–49	25	24
50–59	—2	12
60 or over	6	—1
Gamma over full range of education, all ages combined	.26	.26
Allow speech for government ownership		
Age 30–39	47%	34%
40–49	32	37
50–59	28	41
60 or over	34	0
Gamma over full range of education, all ages combined	.31	.31
Allow book for government ownership in public library		
Age 30–39	42%	35%
40–49	33	42
50–59	16	54
60 or over	34	—4
Gamma over full range of education, all ages combined	.25	.30
Allow proponent of government ownership to teach in a college		
Age 30–39	22%	32%
40–49	20	30
50–59	1	33
60 or over	11	—2
Gamma over full range of education, all ages combined	.04	.16

Table C.2.4. (Cont.)

Civil Liberty	Increase in Prevalence among College Graduates Contrasted with Elementary School Educated	
	NORC	*Gallup Poll*
Allow admitted communist to make speech		
Age 30–39	51%	29%
40–49	35	36
50–59	27	29
60 or over	7	10
Gamma over full range of education, all ages combined	.31	.26
Allow book by admitted communist in public library		
Age 30–39	29%	51%
40–49	50	46
50–59	21	42
60 or over	26	13
Gamma over full range of education, all ages combined	.40	.37
Allow admitted communist to teach in a college		
Age 30–39	10%	13%
40–49	6	17
50–59	6	4
60 or over	20	9
Gamma over full range of education, all ages combined	.14	.11
Allow suspected communist to make speech		
Age 30–39	22%	16%
40–49	17	23
50–59	12	10
60 or over	25	17
Gamma over full range of education, all ages combined	.25	.23
Allow book by suspected communist in public library		
Age 30–39	32%	20%
40–49	17	15
50–59	16	17
60 or over	25	22
Gamma over full range of education, all ages combined	.26	.30
Allow suspected communist to teach in college		
Age 30–39	23%	17%
40–49	16	10
50–59	14	8
60 or over	24	13
Gamma over full range of education, all ages combined	.19	.14

Table C.2.5. The Effects of Education on the Values of Civil Liberties for Nonconformists for Different Generations Enrolled in Institutions at Different Times

Cohort	Level of Education			Effect of College vs. Elementary School	
	Elementary School	High School	College	Absolute Difference	Difference Divided by Maximum Possible
	Mean Percentage Supporting Liberty on Nine Items of Stouffer Scale				
Age 30–39 in					
1954[a]	23 (121)[d]	37 (183)	66 (60)	43%	.51
1974[b]	44 (14)	61 (113)	86 (38)	42	.75
Age 40–49 in					
1954	21 (171)	37 (119)	54 (45)	33	.42
1974	51 (25)	59 (75)	85 (40)	34	.69
Age 50–59 in					
1954	24 (180)·	33 (55)	40 (23)	16	.21
1974	36 (45)	47 (72)	76 (26)	40	.63
Age over 60 in					
1954[f]	20 (305)	30 (64)	42 (13)	22	.28
1974[g]	28 (55)	52 (36)	52 (18)	24	.33
	Percentage Opposed to Banning Atheist's Book from Public Library				
Age 25–36 in					
1964[c]	38 (8)[e]	81 (98)	92 (25)	54%	.87
1974[b]	33 (9)	66 (128)	89 (82)	56	.84
Age 37–48 in					
1964	43 (28)	74 (169)	91 (79)	48	.87
1974	61 (18)	64 (112)	98 (47)	37	.95
Age 49–60 in					
1964	51 (35)	71 (163)	91 (42)	40	.82
1974	42 (31)	49 (81)	77 (30)	35	.60
Age 61–72 in					
1964	44 (52)	73 (67)	71 (21)	27	.48
1974	22 (36)	51 (35)	64 (25)	42	.54

[a]NORC Stouffer survey.
[b]NORC General Social Survey.
[c]NORC 760.
[d]Grade 8 or less.
[e]Grade 8.
[f]60 or over.
[g]60–69.

Table C.2.6. Changes in the Effects of Education on the Values of Civil Liberties for Nonconformists as Cohorts Age by Twenty Years

Civil Liberty	Percentage Supporting Liberty			Relationship over Full Range of Variables	
	Elementary School[a]	High School	College	p	γ
Allow speech against religion					
Age 30–39 in					
1954 NORC survey	24 (121)	50 (183)	77 (60)	***	.45
50–59 in					
1974 NORC survey	40 (45)	54 (72)	73 (26)	ns	.28
Change	+16	+4	−4		
Age 40–49 in					
1954 NORC survey	19 (171)	38 (119)	67 (45)	***	.43
60–69 in					
1974 NORC survey	24 (55)	56 (36)	67 (18)	***	.50
Change	+5	+18	0		
Allow book against religion in public library					
Age 30–39 in					
1954 NORC survey	19 (121)	47 (183)	78 (60)	***	.47
50–59 in					
1974 NORC survey	38 (45)	44 (72)	77 (26)	***	.38
Change	+19	−3	−1		
Age 40–49 in					
1954 NORC survey	20 (171)	45 (119)	67 (45)	***	.42
60–69 in					
1974 NORC survey	22 (55)	61 (36)	56 (18)	**	.36
Change	+2	+16	−11		
Allow antagonist of religion to teach in a college					
Age 30–39 in					
1954 NORC survey	3 (121)	13 (183)	45 (60)	***	.48
50–59 in					
1974 NORC survey	22 (45)	22 (72)	65 (26)	**	.31
Change	+19	+9	+20		
Age 40–49 in					
1954 NORC survey	6 (171)	15 (119)	31 (45)	***	.37
60–69 in					
1974 NORC survey	9 (55)	25 (36)	33 (18)	*	.42
Change	+3	+10	+2		
Allow speech for government ownership					
Age 30–39 in					
1954 NORC survey	50 (121)	65 (183)	97 (60)	***	.36
50–59 in					
1974 NORC survey	60 (45)	71 (72)	92 (26)	ns	.25
Change	+10	+6	−5		

[a]Elementary school equals grades 1–8.

Table C.2.6. (Cont.)

Civil Liberty	Percentage Supporting Liberty			Relationship over Full Range of Variables	
	Elementary School[a]	High School	College	p	γ
Age 40–49 in					
1954 NORC survey	48 (171)	69 (119)	80 (45)	***	.28
60–69 in					
1974 NORC survey	47 (55)	72 (36)	67 (18)	*	.30
Change	−1	+3	−13		
Allow book for government ownership in public library					
Age 30–39 in					
1954 NORC survey	40 (121)	61 (183)	82 (60)	***	.31
50–59 in					
1974 NORC survey	47 (45)	68 (72)	92 (26)	*	.36
Change	+7	+7	+10		
Age 40–49 in					
1954 NORC survey	40 (171)	62 (119)	73 (45)	***	.28
60–69 in					
1974 NORC survey	38 (55)	75 (36)	56 (18)	*	.29
Change	−2	+13	−17		
Allow proponent of government ownership to teach in a college					
Age 30–39 in					
1954 NORC survey	31 (121)	36 (183)	53 (60)	**	.08
50–59 in					
1974 NORC survey	42 (45)	43 (72)	81 (26)	ns	.20
Change	+11	+7	+28		
Age 40–49 in					
1954 NORC survey	27 (171)	35 (119)	47 (45)	*	.12
60–69 in					
1974 NORC survey	35 (55)	42 (36)	39 (18)	ns	.08
Change	+8	+7	−8		
Allow admitted communist to make speech					
Age 30–39 in					
1954 NORC survey	17 (121)	26 (183)	68 (60)	***	.39
50–59 in					
1974 NORC survey	29 (45)	53 (70)	73 (26)	*	.33
Change	+12	+27	+5		
Age 40–49 in					
1954 NORC survey	16 (171)	26 (119)	51 (45)	***	.34
60–69 in					
1974 NORC survey	26 (55)	56 (36)	50 (18)	**	.37
Change	+10	+30	−1		

Table C.2.6. (Cont.)

Civil Liberty	Percentage Supporting Liberty			Relationship over Full Range of Variables	
	Elementary[a] School	High School	College	p	γ
Allow book by admitted communist in public library					
Age 30–39 in 1954 NORC survey	12 (121)	32 (183)	73 (60)	***	.47
50–59 in 1974 NORC survey	24 (45)	45 (71)	81 (26)	***	.39
Change	+12	+13	+8		
Age 40–49 in 1954 NORC survey	12 (171)	36 (119)	62 (45)	***	.43
60–69 in 1974 NORC survey	31 (55)	58 (36)	50 (18)	ns	.28
Change	+19	+22	−12		
Allow admitted communist to teach in a college					
Age 30–39 in 1954 NORC survey	7 (121)	7 (183)	17 (60)	**	.11
50–59 in 1974 NORC survey	20 (45)	26 (70)	50 (26)	ns	.24
Change	+13	+19	+33		
Age 40–49 in 1954 NORC survey	5 (171)	7 (119)	11 (45)	ns	.16
60–69 in 1974 NORC survey	16 (55)	25 (36)	50 (18)	ns	.22
Change	+11	+18	+39		

Mean percentage on all nine items				Effect of College vs. Elementary School	
				Difference	Difference Divided by Maximum Possible
Age 30–39 in 1954 survey	23	37	66	43	.56
50–59 in 1974 survey	36	47	76	40	.63
Change	+13	+10	+10		
Age 40–49 in 1954 survey	21	37	54	33	.42
60–69 in 1974 survey	28	52	52	24	.33
Change	+7	+15	−2		

Table C.2.7. The Effects of Education on the Value of Civil Liberties for Non-conformists as Related to Personal Sympathies

Civil Liberty	Increase in Prevalence among College Graduates Contrasted with Elementary School Group	Relationship over Full Range of Education	
		p	γ
1974 survey[a]			
Allow speech against religion			
Frequent churchgoers[b]	39%	***	.42
Infrequent churchgoers[b]	55	***	.52
Allow book against religion in library			
Frequent churchgoers	48	***	.50
Infrequent churchgoers	47	***	.44
Allow antagonist of religion to teach in a college			
Frequent churchgoers	35	***	.41
Infrequent churchgoers	57	***	.40
1964 survey[c]			
Allow book by admitted atheist in library			
Frequent churchgoers	45%	***	.43
Infrequent churchgoers	42	***	.46
Allow admitted atheist to teach in public high school			
Frequent churchgoers	27	**	.23
Infrequent churchgoers	47	***	.44
Allow admitted atheist to hold public office			
Frequent churchgoers	22	***	.23
Infrequent churchgoers	49	***	.41
1974 survey[a]			
Allow speech for government ownership "Communism worst form of government" [e]			
Those agreeing	26%	ns	.18
Those disagreeing	16	**	.45
Allow book for government ownership in library "Communism worst form of government"			
Those agreeing	42	**	.25
Those disagreeing	35	***	.54

[a]NORC General Social Survey—spring 1974.

[b]Two or three times a month or more often is "frequent"; once a month or less is "infrequent."

[c]NORC 760—October 1964.

Table C.2.7. (Cont.)

Civil Liberty	Increase in Prevalence among College Graduates Contrasted with Elementary School Group	Relationship over Full Range of Education	
		p	γ
Allow antagonist of private ownership to teach in a college			
"Communism worst form of government"			
Those agreeing	36	*	.19
Those disagreeing	17	ns	.25
Allow admitted communist to make speech			
"Communism worst form of government"e			
Those agreeing	42%	**	.30
Those disagreeing	35	***	.48
Allow book by admitted communist in library			
"Communism worst form of government"			
Those agreeing	50	***	.37
Those disagreeing	32	**	.42
Allow admitted communist to teach in a college			
"Communism worst form of government"			
Those agreeing	31	**	.23
Those disagreeing	30	*	.28
*1954 survey*d			
Allow speech against private ownership			
Those believing communists "very great danger"f	41%	***	.29
Others	39	***	.32
Allow book against private ownership in library			
Those believing communists "very great danger"	21	**	.16
Others	42	***	.32

dNORC half of Stouffer survey.

eAfter hearing the statement, "Thinking about all the different kinds of governments in the world today, which of these statements comes closest to how you feel about communism as a form of government?" respondents were given the four statements: "It's the worst kind of all"; "It's bad but no worse than some others"; "It's all right for some countries"; "It's a good form of government."

fThe question read: "How great a danger do you feel American communists are to this country at the present time?" "A very great danger; a great danger; some danger; hardly any danger; or no danger?"

Table C.2.7. (Cont.)

Civil Liberty	Increase in Prevalence among College Graduates Contrasted with Elementary School Group	Relationship over Full Range of Education	
		p	γ
Allow antagonist of private ownership to teach in a college			
Those believing communists "very great danger"	8	ns	.01
Others	23	***	.06
Allow admitted communist to make speech			
Those believing communists "very great danger"	34	***	.39
Others	54	***	.42
Allow book by admitted communist in library			
Those believing communists "very great danger"	34	***	.39
Others	54	***	.42
Allow admitted communist to teach in a college			
Those believing communists "very great danger"	1	ns	.13
Others	15	***	.15

Table C.2.8. The Effects of Education on the Value of Liberty for Public Expression in the Early 1970s

	Percentage Supporting Liberty			Relationship over Full Range of Variables	
Liberty	Elementary School	High School	College	p	γ
1. *Always allow minority to criticize governmental decision favored by majority*[a]					
Age 25–36	54 (13)	63 (115)	92 (64)	***	.52
37–48	63 (24)	66 (104)	93 (40)	***	.42
49–60	35 (26)	64 (69)	86 (22)	***	.47
61–72	40 (55)	66 (44)	61 (18)	**	.32
2. *Always allow people to circulate petitions for governmental action*[a]					
Age 25–36	77 (13)	69 (115)	92 (64)	***	.41
37–48	71 (24)	60 (103)	93 (40)	**	.33
49–60	42 (26)	65 (69)	86 (22)	ns	.34
61–72	42 (55)	61 (44)	67 (18)	ns	.32
3. *Always allow people to hold peaceful demonstrations for governmental action*[a]					
Age 25–36	62 (13)	42 (115)	81 (64)	***	.38
37–48	50 (24)	38 (103)	83 (40)	***	.33
49–60	42 (26)	49 (69)	86 (22)	**	.24
61–72	31 (55)	46 (44)	67 (18)	**	.14
Mean percentage (items 1–3)					
Age 25–36	64	58	88		
37–48	61	55	90		
49–60	40	59	86		
61–72	38	58	65		
4. *Always allow people to block government building for governmental action*[a]					
Age 25–36	8 (13)	3 (115)	6 (64)	ns	.10
37–48	8 (24)	3 (103)	8 (40)	ns	—.02
49–60	4 (26)	3 (69)	0 (22)	ns	—.23
61–72	2 (55)	5 (44)	0 (18)	ns	—.22

[a]NORC 4119—March 1971; elementary school equals grade 8.

Table C.3.1. The Effects of Education on the Value of Freedom
of Information about Birth Control

Cohort	Percentage for Freedom of Information			Relationship over Full Range of Variables	
	Elementary School	High School	College	p	γ
Late 1950s[a]					
Age 25–36	83 (30)	76 (152)	84 (45)	ns	.14
37–48	71 (41)	79 (120)	100 (30)	**	.38
49–60	82 (60)	65 (51)	87 (23)	**	.06
61–72	62 (69)	73 (26)	77 (13)	ns	.21
Early 1960s[b]					
Age 25–36 1962 survey	63 (16)	85 (148)	91 (53)	ns	.34
1964 survey	80 (15)	88 (139)	98 (47)	ns	.25
37–48 1962 survey	53 (32)	79 (122)	78 (36)	ns	.19
1964 survey	74 (35)	91 (147)	91 (55)	*	.33
49–60 1962 survey	73 (51)	77 (53)	70 (30)	ns	.06
1964 survey	64 (42)	94 (65)	82 (27)	**	.31
61–72 1962 survey	54 (54)	73 (44)	92 (12)	ns	.28
1964 survey	82 (50)	77 (34)	86 (21)	ns	.21
Early 1970s[c]					
Age 25–36 1974 survey	100 (9)	95 (128)	100 (82)	ns	.31
1975 survey	71 (7)	99 (127)	100 (81)	***	.80
37–48 1974 survey	83 (18)	96 (112)	94 (47)	ns	.06
1975 survey	82 (11)	96 (100)	94 (48)	*	.27
49–60 1974 survey	84 (31)	94 (81)	97 (30)	**	.52
1975 survey	70 (27)	90 (88)	96 (24)	*	.23
61–72 1974 survey	78 (36)	94 (35)	88 (25)	**	.45
1975 survey	74 (35)	91 (46)	100 (16)	*	.55

[a]Gallup 621K—December 1959; elementary school equals grade 8.

[b]Gallup 662—August 1962; elementary school equals grade 8.

  Gallup 702—November 1964; elementary school equals grade 8.

[c]NORC General Social Surveys—spring 1974 and 1975; elementary school equals grade 8.

Table C.3.2. The Differential Effects of Education on the Value of Freedom of Information about Birth Control for Protestants versus Catholics

	Protestants			Catholics		
Year of Survey	Increased Prevalence in College vs. Elementary School	χ^2	γ	Increased Prevalence in College vs. Elementary School	χ^2	γ
1959	16%	***	.29	—7%	ns	—.12
1962	24	***	.35	—8	ns	.04
1964	16	***	.36	16	ns	.15
1974	13	***	.52	8	ns	.11
1975	28	***	.59	14	**	.38

Table C.4.1. The Effects of Education on the Value of Freedom for Individuals to Intermarry

	Percentage Supporting Freedom			Relationship over Full Range of Variables	
Cohort	Elementary School	High School	College	p	γ
Early 1960s					
Age 25–36 1963 survey[a]	31 (35)	47 (128)	70 (40)	**	.34
1964 survey[b]	23 (13)	42 (78)	80 (25)	**	.43
37–48 1963 survey	16 (62)	43 (101)	75 (36)	***	.51
1964 survey	27 (44)	41 (170)	85 (79)	***	.60
49–60 1963 survey	21 (83)	31 (45)	57 (28)	**	.37
1964 survey	13 (62)	41 (164)	64 (42)	***	.49
61–72 1963 survey	10 (94)	33 (18)	75 (8)	***	.51
1964 survey	24 (97)	36 (66)	73 (22)	***	.43
End of 1960s					
Age 25–36 April 1970[c]	39 (13)	46 (116)	85 (48)	***	.46
September 1970[d]	55 (11)	53 (122)	82 (68)	***	.48
37–48 April 1970	19 (37)	45 (94)	63 (24)	***	.45
September 1970	47 (45)	59 (121)	87 (46)	***	.36
49–60 April 1970	28 (61)	55 (84)	67 (27)	***	.39
September 1970	43 (63)	46 (96)	83 (18)	**	.20
61–72 April 1970	22 (92)	46 (46)	100 (12)	***	.41
September 1970	39 (85)	49 (53)	47 (19)	ns	.11
Early 1970s					
Age 25–36 1974 survey[e]	67 (9)	72 (128)	98 (82)	***	.63
1975 survey[f]	29 (7)	68 (127)	95 (80)	***	.57
37–48 1974 survey	33 (18)	71 (112)	98 (47)	***	.60
1975 survey	36 (11)	60 (100)	96 (48)	***	.55
49–60 1974 survey	39 (31)	51 (80)	83 (30)	***	.41
1975 survey	26 (27)	49 (88)	75 (24)	***	.47
61–72 1974 survey	31 (36)	53 (34)	72 (25)	***	.43
1975 survey	29 (35)	48 (46)	94 (16)	***	.40

[a]NORC 330—December 1963; elementary school equals grades 1–8.

[b]NORC 760—October 1964; elementary school equals grades 0–8.

[c]NORC 4100—elementary school equals grades 0–8.

[d]Gallup 812—elementary school equals grades 0–8.

[e]NORC General Social Survey—spring 1974; elementary school equals grade 8.

[f]NORC General Social Survey—spring 1975; elementary school equals grade 8.

Table C.4.2. Changes in the Effects of Education on the Value of Freedom for Individuals to Intermarry, as Cohorts Age

Cohort	Percentage Supporting Freedom			Relationship over Full Range of Variables	
	Elementary School	High School	College	p	γ
Age 25–36 in					
1965 Gallup survey[a]	25 (12)	56 (139)	72 (47)	***	.41
30–41 in					
1970 Gallup survey[b]	60 (15)	55 (103)	75 (47)	***	.40
Change	35	—1	3		
Age 37–48 in					
1965 Gallup survey	41 (32)	50 (113)	73 (37)	***	.40
42–53 in					
1970 Gallup survey	48 (29)	60 (115)	88 (40)	**	.33
Change	7	10	15		
Age 49–60 in					
1965 Gallup survey	22 (55)	50 (88)	50 (18)	***	.26
54–65 in					
1970 Gallup survey	49 (53)	37 (81)	82 (17)	***	.11
Change	27	—13	32		
Age 25–36 in					
1970 NORC survey[c]	39 (13)	46 (116)	85 (48)	***	.46
29–40 in					
1974 NORC survey[d]	33 (18)	73 (131)	98 (50)	***	.63
Change	—6	27	13		
Age 37–48 in					
1970 NORC survey	19 (37)	45 (94)	63 (24)	***	.45
41–52 in					
1974 NORC survey	39 (33)	58 (95)	94 (46)	***	.54
Change	20	13	31		
Age 49–60 in					
1970 NORC survey	28 (61)	55 (84)	67 (27)	***	.39
53–64 in					
1974 NORC survey	37 (52)	57 (61)	88 (24)	**	.34
Change	9	2	21		

[a]Gallup 705—January 1965; elementary school equals grade 8.

[b]Gallup 812—September 1970; elementary school equals grade 8.

[c]NORC 4100—April 1970; elementary school equals grades 0–8.

[d]NORC General Social Survey—spring 1974; elementary school equals grades 0–8.

Table C.5. The Effects of Education on the Value of
Privacy and Protection from Wiretapping

Cohort	Percentage Supporting Privacy			Relationship over Full Range of Variables	
	Elementary School	High School	College	p	γ
Not fair to use evidence based on wiretapping Early 1950s					
Age 25–36 half-sample 1949[a]	49 (33)	48 (94)	55 (38)	ns	—.11
equivalent half[a]	25 (36)	50 (114)	38 (34)	**	—.07
37–48 half-sample 1949	55 (53)	44 (57)	42 (43)	ns	—.08
equivalent half	43 (53)	29 (63)	33 (43)	**	—.11
49–60 half-sample 1949	48 (46)	44 (41)	48 (25)	ns	—.08
equivalent half	51 (45)	46 (41)	59 (27)	*	—.03
61–72 half-sample 1949	47 (32)	42 (12)	46 (11)	ns	—.11
equivalent half	41 (29)	50 (20)	33 (12)	ns	—.03
25–36 1950 survey[b]	18 (34)	11 (105)	10 (52)	***	—.20
37–48 1950 survey	24 (59)	10 (90)	0 (44)	***	—.27
49–60 1950 survey	26 (76)	8 (37)	0 (24)	***	—.32
61–72 1950 survey	20 (50)	0 (13)	0 (13)	***	—.49
Disapprove of wiretapping Late 1960s					
Age 25–36[c]	43 (7)	48 (139)	51 (59)	ns	.02
37–48	47 (17)	42 (120)	37 (27)	ns	—.10
49–60	50 (28)	42 (71)	41 (27)	ns	—.12
61–72	37 (30)	46 (26)	23 (22)	ns	—.11
Early 1970s					
Age 25–36 1974 survey[d]	78 (9)	77 (127)	81 (82)	ns	—.01
1975 survey[e]	100 (7)	82 (126)	77 (81)	ns	—.19
37–48 1974 survey	83 (18)	80 (112)	70 (47)	***	—.24
1975 survey	91 (11)	81 (99)	77 (48)	*	—.20
49–60 1974 survey	77 (31)	75 (81)	70 (30)	**	—.08
1975 survey	82 (27)	85 (89)	70 (23)	ns	—.21
61–72 1974 survey	67 (36)	66 (35)	64 (25)	ns	—.15
1975 survey	83 (35)	72 (46)	50 (16)	*	—.23

[a]Gallup 443—Forms K and T, June 1949; elementary school equals grades 7–8.

[b]Gallup 452—January 1950; elementary school equals grades 7–8.

[c]Gallup 785—July 1969; elementary school equals grade 8.

[d]NORC General Social Survey—spring 1974; elementary school equals grade 8.

[e]NORC General Social Survey—spring 1975; elementary school equals grade 8.

Table C.6. The Effects of Education on the Value of Equality of Economic and Social Opportunity for Blacks in the 1960s

Opportunity	Percentage Supporting Equality			Relationship over Full Range of Variables	
	Elementary School	High School	College	p	γ
Early 1960s *Blacks should have equal* *chance to get any kind of job*[a]					
Age 25–36	83 (35)	88 (128)	98 (40)	*	.33
37–48	73 (62)	93 (100)	97 (36)	***	.51
49–60	69 (83)	93 (45)	86 (28)	**	.42
61–72	67 (95)	94 (18)	100 (8)	ns	.48
Blacks should have right to *use same parks, restaurants,* *and hotels*[a]					
Age 25–36	69 (35)	75 (126)	93 (40)	ns	.29
37–48	48 (62)	84 (101)	89 (36)	***	.48
49–60	53 (83)	87 (45)	86 (28)	**	.46
61–72	55 (92)	65 (17)	75 (8)	ns	.20
Late 1960s *Blacks should have equal* *chance to get any kind* *of job*[b]					
Age 25–36	81 (21)	92 (132)	96 (54)	**	.43
37–48	82 (39)	87 (135)	96 (50)	ns	.12
49–60	81 (52)	91 (76)	97 (32)	**	.41
61–72	69 (39)	89 (35)	94 (18)	ns	.36
Blacks should have right to *use same parks, restaurants,* *and hotels*[c]					
Age 25–36	77 (13)	96 (116)	96 (46)	*	.40
37–48	54 (37)	87 (94)	92 (24)	***	.46
49–60	66 (62)	89 (84)	96 (27)	**	.54
61–72	70 (91)	85 (46)	100 (12)	**	.49

[a]NORC 330—December 1963; elementary school equals grades 1–8.
[b]NORC 889A—June 1966; elementary school equals grade 8.
[c]NORC 4100—April 1970; elementary school equals 0–8.

Table C.7.1. The Effects of Education on the Value of Equality of Political Opportunity for Minorities in the Late 1950s

Political Opportunity	Percentage Supporting Equality			Relationship over Full Range of Variables	
	Elementary School	High School	College	p	γ
Vote for well-qualified black for president nominated by their party[a]					
Age 25–36	54 (24)	51 (118)	65 (34)	ns	.06
37–48	45 (49)	41 (120)	73 (33)	**	.23
49–60	32 (72)	46 (66)	68 (28)	**	.32
61–72	27 (62)	59 (29)	63 (16)	**	.25
Vote for well-qualified Jew for president nominated by their party[a]					
Age 25–36	58 (24)	76 (118)	88 (34)	*	.27
37–48	61 (49)	83 (120)	85 (33)	***	.34
49–60	53 (72)	80 (66)	89 (28)	**	.28
61–72	63 (62)	79 (29)	81 (16)	*	.31
Vote for well-qualified atheist for president nominated by their party[a]					
Age 25–36	8 (24)	21 (116)	47 (34)	*	.10
37–48	22 (49)	21 (119)	46 (33)	ns	.16
49–60	18 (71)	26 (66)	46 (28)	ns	.16
61–72	13 (62)	17 (29)	38 (16)	ns	.03
Vote for well-qualified Catholic for president nominated by their party[a]					
Protestants,					
Age 25–48 combined	47 (43)	69 (146)	72 (39)	*	.21
49–72 combined	52 (95)	58 (64)	73 (30)	ns	.17
Vote for well-qualified woman for president nominated by their party[a]					
Males,					
age 25–48 combined	52 (31)	60 (109)	63 (38)	ns	.00
49–72 combined	65 (69)	62 (47)	75 (28)	ns	.03

[a]Gallup 622—December 1959; elementary school equals grade 8.

Table C.7.2. The Effects of Education on the Value of Equality of
Political Opportunity for Minorities in the Early 1960s

Political Opportunity	Percentage Supporting Equality			Relationship over Full Range of Variables	
	Elementary School	High School	College	p	γ
Vote for well-qualified black for president nominated by their party					
Age 25–36 1963 survey[a]	33 (15)	54 (126)	78 (45)	**	.31
1965 survey[b]	56 (16)	59 (128)	73 (37)	ns	.21
37–48 1963 survey	47 (43)	43 (123)	69 (39)	***	.28
1965 survey	39 (26)	62 (141)	71 (35)	**	.27
49–60 1963 survey	42 (45)	53 (78)	71 (21)	***	.29
1965 survey	41 (56)	63 (71)	69 (26)	**	.32
61–72 1963 survey	25 (60)	34 (41)	53 (17)	ns	.19
1965 survey	41 (44)	43 (21)	58 (19)	ns	.17
Vote for well-qualified Jew for president nominated by their party					
Age 25–36 1963 survey	60 (15)	84 (127)	89 (45)	***	.39
1965 survey	63 (16)	91 (128)	97 (37)	**	.39
37–48 1963 survey	70 (43)	88 (123)	92 (39)	***	.49
1965 survey	58 (26)	81 (141)	91 (35)	**	.40
49–60 1963 survey	82 (45)	84 (79)	100 (21)	**	.34
1965 survey	64 (56)	87 (71)	89 (26)	***	.46
61–72 1963 survey	65 (60)	83 (40)	94 (17)	ns	.18
1965 survey	73 (44)	76 (21)	63 (19)	ns	.15
Vote for well-qualified Catholic for president nominated by their party					
Protestants, age 25–48 combined					
1963 survey	76 (38)	86 (171)	92 (51)	***	.29
1965 survey	67 (30)	86 (173)	84 (38)	**	.33
age 49–72 combined					
1963 survey	67 (75)	86 (70)	86 (21)	***	.24
1965 survey	77 (68)	84 (63)	79 (34)	**	.24
Vote for well-qualified woman for president nominated by their party					
Males, age 25–48 combined					
1963 survey	46 (28)	53 (93)	60 (45)	ns	.13
age 49–72 combined					
1963 survey	60 (62)	71 (61)	76 (25)	ns	.22

[a]Gallup 676—August 1963; elementary school equals grade 8.
[b]Gallup 714—July 1965; elementary school equals grade 8.

Table C.7.3. The Effects of Education on the Value of Equality of
Political Opportunity for Minorities in the Late 1960s

Political Opportunity	Percentage Supporting Equality			Relationship over Full Range of Variables	
	Elementary School	High School	College	p	γ
Vote for well-qualified black for president nominated by their party					
Age 25–36 1967 survey[a]	29 (21)	68 (117)	75 (48)	**	.38
1969 survey[b]	36 (11)	67 (151)	89 (71)	***	.26
37–48 1967 survey	23 (31)	62 (141)	67 (42)	***	.42
1969 survey	40 (20)	66 (135)	67 (49)	ns	.08
49–60 1967 survey	29 (48)	55 (77)	71 (28)	**	.33
1969 survey	45 (42)	73 (102)	80 (25)	**	.32
61–72 1967 survey	30 (47)	34 (41)	67 (15)	ns	.25
1969 survey	30 (43)	69 (42)	71 (21)	***	.36
Vote for well-qualified Jew for president nominated by their party					
Age 25–36 1967 survey	57 (21)	91 (117)	98 (48)	***	.52
1969 survey	64 (11)	91 (151)	99 (71)	**	.49
37–48 1967 survey	58 (31)	91 (141)	93 (42)	***	.43
1969 survey	53 (19)	94 (135)	92 (49)	***	.44
49–60 1967 survey	73 (48)	83 (77)	93 (28)	*	.34
1969 survey	67 (42)	90 (102)	100 (25)	***	.47
61–72 1967 survey	70 (47)	90 (41)	93 (15)	*	.28
1969 survey	74 (43)	95 (42)	86 (21)	ns	.33
Vote for well-qualified Catholic for president nominated by their party					
Protestants, age 25–48 combined					
1967 survey	86 (36)	93 (162)	93 (56)	***	.31
1969 survey	67 (18)	92 (172)	95 (77)	*	.29
age 49–72 combined					
1967 survey	70 (63)	89 (78)	94 (31)	*	.41
1969 survey	60 (58)	87 (92)	93 (28)	***	.49
Vote for well-qualified woman for president nominated by their party					
Males, age 25–48 combined					
1967 survey	54 (28)	58 (96)	56 (55)	ns	—.11
1969 survey	32 (19)	55 (120)	62 (76)	ns	.07
age 49–72 combined					
1967 survey	54 (56)	77 (62)	86 (28)	*	.26
1969 survey	63 (41)	51 (80)	59 (32)	ns	—.07

[a]Gallup 744—April 1967; elementary school equals grade 8.

[b]Gallup 776—March 1969; elementary school equals grade 8.

Table C.7.4. The Effects of Education on the Value of Equality of Political Opportunity for Minorities in the Early 1970s

Political Opportunity	Percentage Supporting Equality			Relationship over Full Range of Variables	
	Elementary School	High School	College	p	γ
Vote for well-qualified black for president nominated by their party					
Age 25–36 1974 survey	89 (9)	83 (127)	93 (82)	ns	.19
1975 survey	57 (7)	77 (127)	93 (81)	**	.33
37–48 1974 survey	83 (18)	81 (112)	92 (47)	ns	.13
1975 survey	55 (11)	80 (100)	88 (48)	*	.25
49–60 1974 survey	61 (31)	83 (81)	83 (29)	**	.34
1975 survey	85 (27)	66 (89)	92 (24)	ns	.07
61–72 1974 survey	58 (36)	80 (35)	84 (25)	ns	.35
1975 survey	63 (35)	80 (46)	88 (16)	ns	.19
Vote for well-qualified woman for president nominated by their party					
Males, age 25–48 combined					
1974 survey	80 (15)	80 (83)	91 (70)	ns	.24
1975 survey	57 (7)	83 (92)	91 (69)	**	.44
age 49–72 combined					
1974 survey	75 (36)	71 (44)	84 (37)	ns	.14
1975 survey	86 (28)	81 (53)	92 (26)	ns	.26

Note: NORC General Social Surveys—spring 1974 and 1975 elementary school equals grade 8.

Table C.7.5. Changes in the Effects of Education on the Value of Equality
of Political Opportunity for Minorities, as Cohorts Age

	Percentage Supporting Equality			Relationship over Full Range of Variables	
Political Opportunity	Elementary School	High School	College	p	γ
A. *After seven years of aging* *Vote for well-qualified* *black for president* *nominated by their party*					
Age 25–36 in					
December 1959[a]	54 (24)	51 (118)	65 (34)	ns	.06
32–43 in					
April 1967[b]	16 (25)	63 (135)	70 (50)	***	.43
Change	−38	+12	+5		
Age 37–48 in					
December 1959	45 (49)	41 (120)	73 (33)	**	.23
44–55 in					
April 1967	33 (48)	57 (108)	71 (28)	*	.33
Change	−12	+16	−2		
Age 49–60 in					
December 1959	32 (72)	46 (66)	68 (28)	**	.32
56–67 in					
April 1967	24 (45)	51 (41)	65 (23)	**	.38
Change	−8	+5	−3		
Vote for well-qualified *Jew for president* *nominated by their party* Age 25–36 in					
December 1959[a]	58 (24)	76 (118)	88 (34)	*	.27
32–43 in					
April 1967[b]	52 (25)	88 (135)	96 (50)	***	.48
Change	−6	+12	+8		
Age 37–48 in					
December 1959	61 (49)	83 (120)	85 (33)	***	.34
44–55 in					
April 1967	71 (48)	87 (108)	93 (28)	**	.39
Change	+10	+4	+8		
Age 49–60 in					
December 1959	53 (72)	80 (66)	89 (28)	**	.28
56–67 in					
April 1967	71 (45)	88 (41)	91 (23)	*	.30
Change	+18	+8	+2		

[a]Gallup 622—December 1959; elementary school equals grade 8.
[b]Gallup 744—April 1967; elementary school equals grade 8.

Table C.7.5 (Cont.)

Political Opportunity	Percentage Supporting Equality			Relationship over Full Range of Variables	
	Elementary School	High School	College	p	γ
B. *After nine years of aging Vote for well-qualified black for president nominated by their party*					
Age 25–36 in December 1959a	54 (24)	51 (118)	65 (34)	ns	.06
34–45 in March 1969c	47 (17)	65 (138)	71 (51)	ns	.06
Change	−7	+14	+6		
Age 37–48 in December 1959	45 (49)	41 (120)	73 (33)	**	.23
46–57 in March 1969	36 (36)	77 (108)	80 (30)	***	.41
Change	−9	+36	+7		
Age 49–60 in December 1959	32 (72)	46 (66)	68 (28)	**	.32
58–69 in March 1969	43 (44)	65 (62)	74 (19)	ns	.22
Change	+11	+19	+6		
Vote for well-qualified Jew for president nominated by their party					
Age 25–36 in December 1959	58 (24)	76 (118)	88 (34)	*	.27
34–45 in March 1969	69 (16)	95 (138)	94 (51)	ns	.32
Change	+11	+19	+6		
Age 37–48 in December 1959	61 (49)	83 (120)	85 (33)	***	.34
46–57 in March 1969	61 (36)	92 (108)	97 (30)	***	.57
Change	0	+9	+12		
Age 49–60 in December 1959	53 (72)	80 (66)	89 (28)	**	.28
58–69 in March 1969	73 (44)	92 (62)	84 (19)	ns	.24
Change	+20	+12	−5		

cGallup 776—March 1969; elementary school equals grade 8.

Table C.7.6. The Effects of Education on the Value of Equality of Political Opportunity for Minorities (among voters, All Ages Combined)

Political Opportunity	Increase in Prevalence among College Graduates as Contrasted with Elementary School Group	Relationship of Education over Full Range	
		p	γ
Among those who voted in previous presidential election			
1959 survey[a]			
Vote for qualified candidate, nominated by their party, who is			
Black	31%	***	.25
Jewish	30	***	.32
1967 survey[b]			
Vote for qualified candidate, nominated by their party, who is			
Black	41%	***	.34
Jewish	22	***	.40
1969 survey[c]			
Vote for qualified candidate, nominated by their party, who is			
Black	42%	***	.32
Jewish	22	***	.48

[a]Gallup 622.
[b]Gallup 744.
[c]Gallup 776.

Table C.8.1. The Effects of Education on Humane Values Related to Abortion

Situation	Percentage Supporting Humane Values					Relationship over Full Range of Variables	
	Elementary School		High School		College		
							p	γ
Early 1960s								
1. *Allow legal abortion where mother's health is in danger*								
Age 25–36 1962 survey[a]	75	(16)	79	(148)	87	(52)	ns	.09
1965 survey[b]	69	(62)	86	(222)	89	(104)	***	.25
37–48 1962 survey	72	(32)	75	(122)	83	(36)	ns	.12
1965 survey	90	(69)	88	(246)	92	(103)	*	.16
49–60 1962 survey	84	(51)	83	(53)	83	(30)	ns	.05
1965 survey	60	(157)	83	(165)	98	(47)	***	.33
61–72 1962 survey	61	(54)	82	(44)	67	(12)	ns	.22
1965 survey	60	(176)	67	(94)	86	(44)	***	.40
2. *Allow legal abortion where child may be born deformed*								
Age 25–36 1962 survey	38	(16)	54	(148)	62	(52)	ns	.04
1965 survey	26	(62)	47	(222)	74	(104)	***	.29
37–48 1962 survey	50	(32)	57	(122)	67	(36)	ns	.15
1965 survey	58	(69)	58	(246)	65	(103)	ns	—.02
49–60 1962 survey	55	(51)	64	(52)	67	(30)	ns	.08
1965 survey	52	(157)	57	(166)	83	(47)	**	.13
61–72 1962 survey	43	(54)	66	(44)	75	(12)	*	.18
1965 survey	49	(176)	61	(94)	75	(44)	***	.29
3. *Allow legal abortion where family is too poor to support another child*								
Age 25–36 1962 survey	13	(16)	9	(148)	17	(52)	**	—.11
1965 survey	0	(62)	17	(222)	25	(104)	***	.11
37–48 1962 survey	16	(32)	15	(121)	33	(36)	ns	.19
1965 survey	19	(69)	15	(246)	16	(103)	***	.02
49–60 1962 survey	14	(51)	19	(53)	17	(30)	ns	—.07
1965 survey	17	(157)	16	(166)	34	(47)	***	—.05
61–72 1962 survey	21	(53)	28	(43)	25	(12)	ns	.06
1965 survey	17	(176)	12	(94)	16	(44)	*	—.07
Late 1960s[c]								
1. *Allow legal abortion where mother's health is in danger*								
Age 25–36	69	(13)	87	(126)	88	(72)	ns	.21
37–48	77	(30)	80	(161)	98	(52)	***	.45
49–60	74	(42)	83	(83)	87	(31)	ns	.24
61–72	63	(51)	77	(48)	85	(13)	ns	.21

[a]Gallup 662—August 1962; elementary school equals grade 8.
[b]Gallup 721—December 1965; elementary school equals grade 8.
[c]Gallup 788—September 1969; elementary school equals grade 8.

Table **C.8.1.** (Cont.)

| Situation | Percentage Supporting Humane Values | | | Relationship over Full Range of Variables | |
	Elementary School	High School	College	p	γ
2. *Allow legal abortion where child may be born deformed*					
Age 25–36	54 (13)	60 (126)	67 (72)	ns	.11
37–48	57 (30)	61 (161)	79 (52)	**	.32
49–60	41 (42)	65 (83)	74 (31)	*	.23
61–72	51 (51)	69 (48)	85 (13)	ns	.18
3. *Allow legal abortion where family is too poor to support another child*					
Age 25–36	15 (13)	16 (126)	35 (72)	*	.23
37–48	10 (30)	21 (161)	42 (52)	*	.31
49–60	10 (42)	23 (83)	29 (31)	ns	.14
61–72	24 (51)	23 (48)	39 (13)	ns	.09
4. *Allow legal abortion where no health or financial problems but family does not want another child*					
Age 25–36	8 (13)	9 (126)	24 (72)	**	.34
37–48	3 (30)	10 (161)	29 (52)	*	.29
49–60	5 (42)	18 (83)	19 (31)	ns	.09
61–72	10 (51)	13 (48)	31 (13)	ns	.16
Early 1970s					
1. *Allow legal abortion where mother's health is in danger*					
Age 25–36 1974 survey[d]	89 (9)	91 (128)	96 (82)	***	.13
1975 survey[e]	71 (7)	91 (127)	90 (81)	ns	.13
37–48 1974 survey	83 (18)	93 (112)	89 (47)	ns	—.22
1975 survey	82 (11)	92 (99)	92 (48)	ns	.24
49–60 1974 survey	84 (31)	84 (81)	87 (30)	ns	.00
1975 survey	67 (27)	87 (89)	83 (24)	**	.06
61–72 1974 survey	81 (36)	89 (35)	96 (25)	ns	.28
1975 survey	82 (34)	89 (46)	94 (16)	ns	.22
2. *Allow legal abortion where child may be born deformed*					
Age 25–36 1974 survey	78 (9)	84 (128)	92 (82)	ns	.22
1975 survey	43 (7)	84 (127)	84 (81)	**	.12
37–48 1974 survey	78 (18)	82 (112)	87 (47)	ns	.08
1975 survey	73 (11)	83 (99)	85 (48)	ns	.15

[d]NORC General Social Survey—spring 1974; elementary school equals grade 8.
[e]NORC General Social Survey—spring 1975; elementary school equals grade 8.

Table **C.8.1.** (Cont.)

Situation	Percentage Supporting Humane Values						Relationship over Full Range of Variables	
	Elementary School		High School		College		p	γ
49–60 1974 survey	87	(31)	82	(81)	83	(30)	ns	.08
1975 survey	67	(27)	84	(89)	83	(24)	ns	.10
61–72 1974 survey	72	(36)	91	(35)	92	(25)	ns	.23
1975 survey	71	(35)	87	(46)	88	(16)	ns	.40
3. *Allow legal abortion where family is too poor to support another child*								
Age 25–36 1974 survey	33	(9)	50	(128)	74	(82)	**	.37
1975 survey	14	(7)	49	(127)	65	(81)	**	.35
37–48 1974 survey	22	(18)	47	(112)	68	(47)	*	.34
1975 survey	9	(11)	56	(99)	71	(48)	**	.33
49–60 1974 survey	42	(31)	57	(81)	57	(30)	ns	.18
1975 survey	33	(27)	46	(89)	67	(24)	ns	.19
61–72 1974 survey	47	(36)	54	(35)	52	(25)	ns	.23
1975 survey	39	(33)	57	(46)	81	(16)	ns	.26
4. *Allow legal abortion where family does not want another child*								
Age 25–36 1974 survey	56	(9)	40	(128)	68	(82)	**	.35
1975 survey	14	(7)	45	(127)	62	(81)	*	.31
37–48 1974 survey	22	(18)	41	(112)	68	(47)	**	.35
1975 survey	9	(11)	52	(99)	67	(48)	**	.29
49–60 1974 survey	26	(31)	48	(81)	57	(30)	ns	.29
1975 survey	22	(27)	33	(89)	63	(24)	ns	.15
61–72 1974 survey	33	(36)	43	(35)	40	(25)	ns	.23
1975 survey	20	(35)	52	(46)	69	(16)	*	.30
5. *Allow legal abortion where mother single and does not want to marry the man*								
Age 25–36 1974 survey	56	(9)	45	(128)	71	(82)	**	.33
1975 survey	0	(7)	46	(127)	65	(81)	***	.40
37–48 1974 survey	22	(18)	44	(112)	68	(47)	**	.39
1975 survey	18	(11)	50	(98)	67	(48)	*	.34
49–60 1974 survey	39	(31)	53	(81)	57	(30)	ns	.23
1975 survey	26	(27)	38	(89)	71	(24)	**	.20
61–72 1974 survey	36	(36)	49	(35)	60	(25)	ns	.29
1975 survey	24	(33)	61	(46)	69	(16)	*	.36

Table **C.8.1.** (Cont.)

Situation	Percentage Supporting Humane Values			Relationship over Full Range of Variables	
	Elementary School	High School	College	p	γ
6. *Allow legal abortion where woman became pregnant as result of rape*					
Age 25–36 1974 survey	67 (9)	85 (128)	95 (82)	*	.36
1975 survey	57 (7)	84 (127)	89 (81)	**	.35
37–48 1974 survey	67 (18)	79 (112)	87 (47)	ns	.12
1975 survey	64 (11)	83 (99)	88 (48)	ns	.24
49–60 1974 survey	77 (31)	89 (81)	90 (30)	**	.35
1975 survey	56 (27)	82 (89)	88 (24)	**	.24
61–72 1974 survey	75 (36)	91 (35)	92 (25)	ns	.31
1975 survey	74 (34)	89 (46)	88 (16)	ns	.36

Table C.8.2. Mean Prevalence of Support for Legalizing Abortion under Conditions 1–3 among Various Age and Educational Groups in Several Time Periods

Cohort	Mean Percentage Supporting Abortion		
	Elementary School	High School	College
Early 1960s			
Age 25–36	37	49	59
37–48	51	51	59
49–60	47	54	64
61–72	42	53	57
Late 1960s			
Age 25–36	46	54	63
37–48	48	54	73
49–60	42	57	63
61–72	35	56	70
Early 1970s			
Age 25–36	55	75	83
37–48	58	76	82
49–60	63	73	77
61–72	65	78	84

Table C.8.3. The Differential Effects of Education on Humane Values Related to Abortion for Protestants versus Catholics

Situation	Protestants			Catholics		
	Increased Prevalence in College vs. Elementary School	χ^2	γ	Increased Prevalence in College vs. Elementary School	χ^2	γ
Allow abortion where mother's health is endangered						
1962	12%	**	.27	—13%	*	—.17
1965	26	***	.38	23	***	.26
1969[a]	26	***	.64	12	ns	.11
1974	10	***	.27	9	ns	—.08
1975	16	**	.29	7	ns	.09
Allow abortion where child may be born deformed						
1962	20%	*	.08	—19%	**	—.10
1965	32	***	.21	3	*	—.06
1969[a]	45	***	.36	—15	*	—.11
1974	10	ns	.23	6	ns	.05
1975	20	***	.30	11	ns	.05
Allow abortion where family is too poor to support another child						
1962	5%	ns	.05	—21%	ns	—.26
1965	11	***	.00	—17	***	—.32
1969[a]	36	***	.22	—2	ns	—.13
1974	26	***	.31	23	ns	.13
1975	49	***	.33	7	ns	.06

[a]In this survey it was possible to sharpen the contrast. The Protestants examined were *non*churchgoers, and the Catholics were churchgoers.

Table C.9. The Effects of Education on Humane Values Related to Capital Punishment

Opinion on Capital Punishment	Percentage Supporting Humane Values			Relationship over Full Range of Variables	
	Elementary School	High School	College	p	γ
Early 1950s					
1. *Against death penalty for persons convicted of murder*[a]					
Age 25–36	17 (36)	22 (166)	21 (43)	ns	—.10
37–48	19 (92)	26 (114)	15 (34)	ns	—.11
49–60	36 (80)	28 (50)	21 (19)	ns	—.11
61–72	19 (58)	33 (18)	8 (13)	ns	.09
2. *Favor death penalty generally, but against it for those under 21 convicted of murder*[a]					
Age 25–36	52 (31)	59 (150)	58 (38)	ns	.08
37–48	47 (79)	57 (96)	65 (31)	ns	.11
49–60	66 (67)	56 (43)	63 (19)	ns	—.09
61–72	50 (50)	50 (14)	58 (12)	ns	.03
Late 1950s					
1. *Against death penalty for persons convicted of murder*[b]					
Age 25–36	16 (32)	27 (131)	33 (39)	ns	—.04
37–48	30 (69)	34 (103)	44 (45)	ns	—.02
49–60	30 (98)	40 (50)	36 (22)	ns	.06
61–72	33 (70)	19 (21)	50 (16)	ns	—.03
2. *Favor death penalty generally, but against it for teenager convicted of murder*[b]					
Age 25–36	42 (24)	57 (89)	53 (32)	ns	.06
37–48	54 (43)	46 (72)	64 (28)	ns	—.03
49–60	49 (67)	63 (30)	50 (12)	ns	.13
61–72	65 (43)	65 (17)	75 (12)	ns	—.02
Early 1960s					
1. *Against death penalty for persons convicted of murder*[c]					
Age 25–36	50 (12)	33 (88)	44 (36)	ns	—.01

[a]Gallup 522—October 1953; elementary school equals grades 7–8.
[b]Gallup 588—August 1957; elementary school equals grades 7–8.
[c]Gallup 704—January 1965; elementary school equals grade 8.

Table C.9. (Cont.)

Opinion on Capital Punishment	Percentage Supporting Humane Values			Relationship over Full Range of Variables	
	Elementary School	High School	College	p	γ
37–48	53 (30)	39 (101)	49 (33)	ns	.01
49–60	25 (24)	32 (50)	37 (27)	ns	—.04
61–72	52 (27)	21 (24)	44 (9)	**	.00
2. Favor death penalty generally, but against it for those under 21 convicted of murder[c]					
Age 25–36	d	60 (47)	26 (19)	ns	—.17
37–48	23 (13)	53 (55)	47 (15)	ns	.23
49–60	36 (14)	65 (26)	46 (13)	ns	.01
61–72	20 (10)	33 (18)	d	ns	.05
3. Against death penalty for worst crimes[e]					
Age 25–36	25 (8)	40 (97)	44 (25)	ns	.04
37–48	48 (27)	38 (170)	39 (78)	ns	.05
49–60	46 (35)	42 (164)	29 (42)	ns	—.02
61–72	31 (52)	42 (67)	46 (22)	ns	.16
Late 1960s					
1. Against death penalty for persons convicted of murder[f]					
Age 25–36	27 (11)	32 (140)	51 (53)	ns	.13
37–48	48 (27)	33 (126)	36 (60)	ns	—.20
49–60	33 (55)	39 (82)	34 (32)	ns	.02
61–72	41 (44)	34 (41)	59 (17)	ns	—.01
Early 1970s					
1. Against death penalty for persons convicted of murder					
Age 25–36					
1972 Gallup survey[g]	40 (10)	46 (121)	48 (61)	ns	—.01
1972 NORC survey[h]	71 (7)	33 (125)	49 (78)	**	—.03
1974 NORC survey[i]	11 (9)	21 (127)	42 (82)	ns	.25

[d]Too few cases to report percentage.

[e]NORC 760—October 1964; elementary school equals grade 8.

[f]Gallup 746—May 1967, elementary school equals grade 8.

[g]Gallup 846—February 1972; elementary school equals grade 8.

[h]NORC General Social Survey—spring 1972; elementary school equals grade 8.

[i]NORC General Social Survey—spring 1974; elementary school equals grade 8.

Table C.9. (Cont.)

Opinion on Capital Punishment	Percentage Supporting Humane Values			Relationship over Full Range of Variables	
	Elementary School	High School	College	p	γ
37–48					
1972 Gallup survey	40 (15)	33 (95)	47 (47)	ns	.09
1972 NORC survey	19 (21)	32 (102)	24 (34)	ns	.01
1974 NORC survey	28 (18)	23 (112)	38 (47)	ns	.07
49–60					
1972 Gallup survey	48 (23)	37 (89)	37 (27)	ns	—.02
1972 NORC survey	21 (38)	28 (90)	21 (29)	ns	—.17
1974 NORC survey	19 (31)	21 (81)	33 (30)	ns	.04
61–72					
1972 Gallup survey	46 (46)	25 (36)	24 (17)	ns	—.13
1972 NORC survey	42 (31)	29 (38)	26 (19)	ns	.00
1974 NORC survey	22 (36)	26 (35)	20 (25)	ns	.05

Table C.10. The Effects of Education on Humane Values related to the Regulation of Guns

Cohort	Percentage Supporting Humane Values			Relationship over Full Range of Variables	
	Elementary School	High School	College	p	γ
Late 1950s[a]					
Age 25–36	76 (21)	76 (127)	77 (47)	ns	—.06
37–48	75 (56)	84 (116)	59 (27)	*	—.03
49–60	76 (54)	81 (67)	65 (23)	ns	.03
61–72	62 (66)	73 (30)	80 (5)	ns	.12
Early 1960s[b]					
Age 25–36	42 (12)	69 (88)	83 (36)	*	.23
37–48	70 (30)	76 (101)	67 (33)	*	.00
49–60	58 (24)	78 (50)	74 (27)	ns	.09
61–72	63 (27)	92 (24)	78 (9)	ns	.19
Early 1970s					
Age 25–36					
1972 Gallup survey[c]	69 (13)	64 (126)	74 (74)	**	.12
1974 NORC survey[d]	89 (9)	81 (128)	82 (82)	ns	.06
Age 37–48					
1972 Gallup survey	70 (20)	68 (102)	73 (41)	ns	.07
1974 NORC survey	72 (18)	73 (112)	74 (47)	ns	.04
Age 49–60					
1972 Gallup survey	50 (32)	75 (81)	85 (33)	**	.25
1974 NORC survey	67 (30)	74 (81)	77 (30)	ns	.25
Age 61–72					
1972 Gallup survey	80 (44)	83 (59)	73 (22)	ns	.11
1974 NORC survey	78 (36)	71 (34)	64 (25)	ns	—.05

[a]Gallup 616—July 1959; elementary school equals grade 8.

[b]Gallup 704—January 1965; elementary school equals grade 8.

[c]Gallup 852—May 1972; elementary school equals grade 8.

[d]NORC General Social Survey—spring 1974; elementary school equals grade 8.

Appendix D

Tables Summarizing the Findings When Various
Social Factors Are Controlled

Table D.1. Summary Findings on Effects of Education on Values Relating to Civil Liberties When Various Social Factors Are Controlled (All Periods Combined)

Social Factors	Number of Tests[a] Where χ^2 Is Significant	Number of Tests Where χ^2 Is Not Significant	Mean γ	Number of Tests Where γs Differ by Less Than .10	Number of Tests Where γ Is at Least .10 Higher Than in Contrasted Group
Sex					
Male	51	2	.36	} 34	17
Female	49	4	.30		2
Religion					
Protestant	41	3	.31	} 22	17
Catholic	29	15	.23		5
Native-born[b]	15	0	.32		
Social Origins					
High	19	2	.43	} 12	3
Low	15	6	.47		6
Residential origins					
South	18	0	.39	} 6	4
Non-South	18	0	.43		8
Farm	17	4	.34	} 13	0
City	21	0	.42		8
Current residence					
South	43	6	.31	} 35	8
Non-South	48	1	.32		6
Breadwinner's current occupation					
Professional or managerial	44	9	.38	} 12	37
Blue-collar	34	19	.22		4

[a]$p \leq .05$.

[b]The variation in the number of controlled tests arises because some surveys did not record a particular social characteristic.

Table D.2. Summary Findings on Effects of Education on the Value of Freedom of Information When Various Social Factors Are Controlled (All Periods Combined)

Social Factors	Number of Tests[a] Where χ^2 Is Significant	Number of Tests Where χ^2 Is Not Significant	Mean γ	Number of Tests Where γs Differ by Less Than .10	Number of Tests Where γ Is at Least .10 Higher Than in Contrasted Group
Sex					
Male	5	0	.35	4	0
Female	5	0	.36		1
Social Origins[b]					
High	2	0	.30	0	1
Low	1	1	.42		1
Residential origins					
South	2	0	.59	0	2
Non-South	2	0	.36		0
Farm	2	0	.46	0	1
City	1	1	.37		1
Current residence					
South	5	0	.41	4	1
Non-South	4	1	.29		0
Breadwinner's current occupation					
Professional or managerial	2	3	.24	1	1
Blue-collar	5	0	.32		3

[a]$p \leq .05$.

[b]The variation in the number of controlled tests arises because some surveys did not record a particular social characteristic.

Table D.3. Summary Findings on Effects of Education on the Value of Freedom for Individuals to Intermarry When Various Social Factors Are Controlled (All Periods Combined)

Social Factors	Number of Tests[a] Where χ^2 Is Significant	Number of Tests Where χ^2 Is Not Significant	Mean γ	Number of Tests Where γs Differ by Less Than .10	Number of Tests Where γ Is at Least .10 Higher Than in Contrasted Group
Sex					
Male	6	0	.45	} 5	0
Female	6	0	.50		1
Religion					
Protestant	6	0	.48	} 5	1
Catholic	5	1	.44		0
Native-born[b]	2	0	.49		
Social Origins					
High	4	0	.53	} 2	1
Low	3	1	.44		1
Residential origins					
South	3	0	.45	} 3	0
Non-South	3	0	.47		0
Farm	2	0	.48	} 2	0
City	2	0	.55		0
Current residence					
South	6	0	.55	} 4	2
Non-South	6	0	.46		0
Breadwinner's current occupation					
Professional or managerial	6	0	.53	} 2	4
Blue-collar	4	2	.30		0

[a]$p \leq .05$.

[b]The variation in the number of controlled tests arises because some surveys did not record a particular social characteristic.

Table D.4. Summary Findings on Effects of Education on the Value of Equality of Opportunity for Minorities When Various Social Factors Are Controlled (All Periods Combined)

Social Factors	Number of Tests[a] Where χ^2 Is Significant	Number of Tests Where χ^2 Is Not Significant	Mean γ	Number of Tests Where γs Differ by Less Than .10	Number of Tests Where γ Is at Least .10 Higher Than in Contrasted Group
Sex					
Male	22	0	.34	} 15	4
Female	21	1	.35		3
Religion					
Protestant	15	1	.33	} 9	2
Catholic	8	8	.35		5
Native-born[b]	3	0	.41		
Social Origins					
High	3	1	.26	} 3	1
Low	2	2	.18		0
Residential origins					
South	5	0	.43	} 4	1
Non-South	5	0	.40		0
Farm	2	0	.31	} 1	1
City	0	2	.21		0
Current residence					
South	18	4	.32	} 13	5
Non-South	20	2	.29		4
Breadwinner's current occupation					
Professional or managerial	19	3	.31	} 10	7
Blue-collar	16	6	.27		5

[a] $p \leq .05$.

[b] The variation in the number of controlled tests arises because some surveys did not record a particular social characteristic.

Table D.5. Summary Findings on Effects of Education on Humane Values ⌐ Abortion When Various Social Factors Are Controlled (All Periods Combine

Social Factors	Number of Tests[a] Where χ^2 Is Significant	Number of Tests Where χ^2 Is Not Significant	Mean γ	Number of Tests Where γs Differ by Less Than .10	N T⌐ γ 1 .10 Tha Cont Grou
Sex					
Male	20	2	.21	} 18	2
Female	18	4	.21		2
Social Origins[b]					
High	9	3	.26	} 4	8
Low	3	9	.12		0
Residential origins					
South	9	3	.31	} 8	4
Non-South	9	3	.20		0
Farm	10	2	.25	} 8	3
City	8	4	.21		1
Current residence					
South	15	7	.24	} 11	9
Non-South	14	8	.17		2
Breadwinner's current occupation					
Professional or managerial	14	8	.18	} 12	7
Blue-collar	8	14	.13		3

[a] $p \leq .05$.

[b] The variation in the number of controlled tests arises because some surveys did not record a particular social characteristic.

Notes

Chapter 1 Introduction

1. Herbert H. Hyman, Charles R. Wright, and John Shelton Reed, *The Enduring Effects of Education* (Chicago: University of Chicago Press, 1975; Phoenix paperback, 1978).

2. Kenneth Feldman and Theodore Newcomb, *The Impact of College on Students*, 2 vols. (San Francisco: Jossey-Bass, 1969), 1: 308. Since 1969, Hoge and Bender have followed up other classes of Dartmouth alumni. Theirs is an admirable strategy that by successive increments has built up a substantial body of evidence on change and persistence up to twenty-nine years after college, but the evidence nevertheless is limited to a highly select population of men at one Ivy League college. See Dean R. Hoge and Irving E. Bender, "Factors Influencing Value Change among College Graduates in Adult Life," *Journal of Personality and Social Psychology* 29 (1974): 572–85.

3. The scope of some of the largest studies in the recent literature illustrates the general point. McLeish conducted a longitudinal study of effects on values and attitudes among students enrolled in ten colleges in England, measuring changes from entrance in 1965 to exit in 1968. Farnen and German studied the effects of instruction on the political values and attitudes of some 1,800 students, ranging from nine to twenty years of age, in the schools of five nations. Chickering and his associates examined changes in libertarian values among American students at thirteen colleges from the time of their entrance in 1965 to the end of their sophomore year in 1967. In 1968, Spaeth and Greeley relocated a subsample of about 5,000 members of an earlier national sample of 40,000 college graduates of the class of 1961. Their measurements, combined with a series of earlier measurements spaced between 1961 and 1964, seem to carry us at least a bit of the way toward the study of enduring effects of *college* education, albeit effects specific to that narrow point in the history of educational institutions. But as they properly note: "It is impossible, without being able to make comparisons with those who do not go to college—comparisons in which all other background variables are held constant—to define precisely the impact of higher education." That crucial finding, as they go on to note, is "beyond the scope of our present efforts" (pp. 23–24). Joe L. Spaeth and Andrew M. Greeley, *Recent Alumni and Higher Education: A Survey of College Graduates* (New York: McGraw-Hill, 1970). Jennings and his associates have reported findings on the effects of high-school education on political socialization based on a large nationwide sample of high-school seniors, measured in 1965 during their senior year and interviewed again in 1973. But these findings, however massive and informative, can carry us only to the point when individuals have reached age twenty-five, are limited to the one cohort educated in the particular period, and of course provide no evidence on the effects of fewer than twelve years of school, although subgroup comparisons can test the effects of various additional years of college education. The "National Longitudinal Study" sponsored by the National Center for Education Statistics and the U.S. Office of Education involves a baseline survey of a national sample of more than 20,000 members of the high-school class of 1972 and periodic follow-up surveys originally projected for six to eight years. It may serve its intended purposes of charting the educational, vocational, and personal development of this particular group after high-school, and depending on its extension in time it may ultimately track this one cohort a short distance into adult life. But the study cannot provide any rigorous test of the *effects of high-school* education, more specifically of that one cycle in the history of American high schools, since it

suffers from the same limitations as the Jennings study and the Spaeth and Greeley study. The design lacks a comparison or control group with fewer than twelve years of school. By a series of nationwide surveys of college students and youth not enrolled in colleges, all aged twenty-five or less, Yankelovich has provided large-scale comparative evidence, but once again relevant only to short-term effects of education on values and attitudes. In a series of publications, Astin, Bayer, and Boruch have reported findings on changes in political attitudes and values and their determinants based on the American Council on Education's testing of thousands of students every year, representative of the freshmen population entering colleges throughout the nation. Each of the four freshman classes who entered in the years 1966 through 1969 has been followed up four years later, and subgroup comparisons between those who had more and less exposure to college (but not *zero* exposure, since there is no control group without any college) can reveal *some* of the effects of higher education as it operated in that particular historical period. At best, ignoring these limitations and the possible bias created by a noncompletion rate between 35% and 60%, these studies once again deal only with immediate effects during college. There was, however, one earlier wave of inquiry: a large sample of freshmen who entered in 1961 were followed up four years later and again in 1971. In theory, this would provide evidence on effects that lasted for some years out of college and into early phases of adult life. The variables measured, however, are limited mainly to career plans and occupational attainment. The 1977 monograph reviewing all the studies has a chapter devoted to the "Permanence of College Effects"; the only use made there of the 1961 study is one table that presents *aggregate changes in career choices* over time. Obviously, this analysis in no way demonstrates the influence of college, since there is no comparison finding for those with little or no exposure to college. Astin, understandably, remarks more than once in this chapter that the evidence on long-term effects is "tentative and . . . highly ambiguous" (p. 193). Alexander W. Astin, *Four Critical Years: Effects of College on Beliefs, Attitudes, and Knowledge* (San Francisco: Jossey-Bass, 1977). The National Assessment of Educational Progress, the latest and largest continuing program of research, has been obtaining massive nationwide findings on the effects of education in both the cognitive and value realms but, apart from the samples of students, has included only *young* adults aged twenty-six to thirty-five, thus just beginning to trace enduring effects out to the further reaches of life and being limited to a few cohorts who reflect the schools and environment of a narrow historical period. How little attention is paid to this limitation is suggested by a recent comprehensive study of the National Assessment that was commissioned by the Carnegie Corporation, one of the major sponsors of the National Assessment. In the two hundred pages of this thorough, technically sophisticated, and stringent analysis, there is only one passing allusion to that portion of the study dealing with adults. The allusion, in a footnote, remarks that a graded series of dollar rewards was given to the adult respondents to induce them to complete the exercises. And even the implications of this procedure for the sampling of adults are not commented upon at all. See William Greenbaum, *Measuring Educational Progress* (New York: McGraw-Hill, 1977). Studies of long-term *economic* effects, in contrast with the scarcity just reviewed, are plentiful. A substantial body of data on the differences in earnings and occupational position between adults with more and less education has been analyzed and reanalyzed, and the interpretation of the findings has been hotly debated. Two recent collections of essays illustrate such studies and the disputes and uncertainties that arise from the ambiguities and limitations of the data. F. Thomas Juster, ed., *Education, Income and Human Behavior* (New York: McGraw-Hill. 1975); Lewis C. Solmon and Paul J. Taubman, eds., *Does College Matter? Some Evidence on the Impacts of Higher Education* (New York: Academic Press, 1973). The reader should not be misled by the expansive titles of these works. If he sets aside the effects reported on money and position, savings and consumption, the remaining treatment of enduring noneconomic effects

138

is based on meager or flimsy evidence or on sheer speculation and prejudice. For example, an essay by Ellison and Simon titled "Does College Make a Person Healthy and Wise?" remarks: "Our highly subjective estimate is that the half-life of most factual knowledge and course-specific skills is of the order of several months" (Solmon and Taubman, p. 56). Freeman, a participant in one symposium, faults the positive conclusions of another contributor on the categorical ground that his evidence relates "to attitudes rather than behavior" (Solmon and Taubman, p. 322). Machlup, another contributor, properly cautions that "the valuation of nonpecuniary social benefits is a delicate matter," being based at times on "a single arbiter, with all his personal biases and prejudices concerning societal goals." But he then categorically asserts his own prejudices: "We cannot measure such benefits" and eliminates one line of future research on the ground that "replies to questionnaires would be quite unreliable" (Solman and Taubman, pp. 360–62). Given the weighty, if ambiguous, evidence of economic effects and the flimsy evidence on non-economic effects, investment in education inevitably ends up being measured by its payoff in dollars and cents. However important, this is surely too narrow a criterion.

4. In our first study, although almost all the evidence is based on 54 surveys conducted between 1949 and 1971, a few additional tests of the effects on knowledge were obtained from one survey conducted in 1974.

5. Of course, we could not completely blind ourselves in every instance. The Stouffer 1954 survey on civil liberties, for example, led to a classic book and we could not help knowing the earlier published findings on the relationship between education and the particular values studied. But this survey, like all the others, was included because it was of high quality, fell within the time period to be examined, and measured values highly relevant to our problem; and that decision was firm before we had made any special tabulations.

6. *Enduring Effects of Education*, pp. 32–34, 126; table 1. Evidence was also presented that error in *measurement* of educational attainment is small in magnitude and that the pattern of such error cannot distort the conclusions drawn from our major mode of analysis.

7. Over the long period spanned by our surveys, there has been a rise in the *current* enrollment in educational institutions of adults aged twenty-five to thirty-four, all but an infinitesimal number of them enrolled in *college*. Figures for those aged thirty-five or over are not available before the 1970s, but for whites (nonwhites, as we shall note later, are not included in any of our analyses) aged twenty-five to thirty-four, the census estimates that 2.8% were enrolled in 1955, 3.8% in 1960, 4.9% in 1965, 6.1% in 1970, and 7.7% in 1974. The figures that became available in 1973–74 for those aged thirty-five or over indicate that their rate of enrollment is *considerably less than half* that of those aged twenty-five to thirty-four. It seems reasonable to apply that same ratio to estimate the current enrollment of the older age group in the 1950s and 1960s. Thus, before 1970, almost all the *college*-educated adults we studied were reflecting their *past*, not current, education, and effectively *all* the adults with lower levels of educational attainment were reflecting past exposure. Even in the analysis of the surveys from the 1970s, fewer than 4% of our three older cohorts are reflecting the effects of current education, and for our youngest cohort, aged twenty-five to thirty-six, the greatest bulk—well over 90%—are reflecting past exposure. *Statistical Abstract of the United States, 1977* (Washington, D.C.: Government Printing Office), pp. 133–34, tables 210, 212. *The Condition of Education* (Washington, D.C.: Government Printing Office, 1976) p. 226, table 4.14.

8. In almost all the surveys, age was recorded and coded to the exact year. So it was possible to maintain uniformity across both studies in the life-stages at which the effects of education were examined. However, in three of the surveys used for the study of values, age had been coded into step intervals, and so in these instances the four life-stages that were examined depart from their standard definitions. That variation is small,

the young adults being twenty-five to thirty-four and the middle-aged being thirty-five to forty-four or forty-five to fifty-four in two of these surveys. These departures are carefully noted in the later tables, and wherever the lack of comparability might have affected a conclusion about the differential effects across the surveys and time periods, the life-stages were redefined on the basis of the less refined age data so as to be exactly comparable.

9. It is true, of course, that some adults return to school or college after many years to complete or extend their *formal* education, and in such instances the education cannot be "dated" so easily. However, on the basis of the evidence reviewed in note 7 and other evidence, this pattern characterizes fewer than 5% of adults over the period spanned by our studies, the remainder experiencing all their formal education in the normal sequence during childhood and youth. Thus there is very little error in dating such educational experience and the distance away in years from it solely on the basis of the age of the individuals.

10. *Enduring Effects of Education*, p. 35.

11. To illustrate the pattern of attrition, among whites who had reached ages seventy-five to eighty-four in the 1950s (the early period covered in our studies), the annual death rate was *more than double* that among individuals aged sixty-five to seventy-four. In the latter age group, it was about five thousand per hundred thousand or 5% among males, and about 3% among females. In our younger age cohorts, the rate of attrition is so much lower that any error that might affect our analyses is negligible. Among whites who reached age forty-five to sixty-four in the 1950s, the death rate was about 1.5% among males and about 0.7% among females, and the annual rates were even lower among white adults between the ages of twenty-five and forty-four: 0.10% and 0.3% for females and males respectively. In the later period covered in our studies, the *change* in the rates as people age is of about the same magnitude. For summary data on the 1950s, see Matilda W. Riley and Anne Foner, *Aging and Society* (New York: Russell Sage Foundation, 1968), 1: 196–99. For more detailed data covering a longer period, see *Statistical Abstract of the United States* (Washington: Government Printing Office, 1970), p. 55, table 68.

12. Two other factors may complicate inferences about the sheer effect of aging drawn from unrestricted cohort analyses: the changing sex composition as a cohort ages owing to the greater longevity of women, and the changing ethnic composition owing to past waves of immigration. However, since sex was reported in all the surveys and nativity in many of them, it was possible to control these factors when necessary. It is also true that the socioeconomic composition of a cohort changes with age, since those who are better off are more likely to survive. But our mode of analysis, subdividing the cohort into educational strata that are then compared over the course of aging, automatically provides substantial control over this factor because of the high correlation between educational and economic position, and economic status can also be directly controlled. For a more detailed treatment of the magnitude of the problems and modes of control, see *Enduring Effects of Education*, pp. 9–12, and the discussion below.

13. The nominal identity of questions does not necessarily insure their *functional* equivalence in different historical contexts, and this problem will be reviewed later.

14. As the reader will see later, some specific items were included that are controversial and regarded by many as indicative of undesirable values. But these served such special purposes as testing whether education might create some bad as well as some good effects, sometimes by leading the individual to overextend and apply a good value in such an unqualified and extreme way that the result could be considered undesirable. As a prelude to his recent critical and comprehensive review of all the available evidence on the effects of college education, Bowen confronted all the dilemmas of interpretation that should be anticipated in any such inquiry as his or ours. "Because it is a potent force,

higher education may open up possibilities for bad as well as good outcomes. . . . Some of the results of higher education may be controversial. . . . Many controversial outcomes are beset with semantic confusion. For example, if an outcome of higher education is described as helping to induct students into cosmopolitan culture and to emancipate them from provincialism, the result may be considered beneficial; if the same result is described as alienating young people from their families and the traditions of their local communities or ethnic groups, it may be considered harmful. Moreover, some outcomes are viewed differently at different times according to the social context. For example, in a time of peace and pacifistic sentiments; the discovery of a new biological weapon may be viewed widely as an outrage; in the midst of a desperate war, the same outcome could be regarded as a justifiable expedient." We, like Bowen, have tried to steer a sane and thoughtful course, and one solution we have employed is to study a limited realm, within which there would be much agreement on the "goodness" of the values. See Howard Bowen, *Investment in Learning: The Individual and Social Value of American Higher Education* (San Francisco: Jossey-Bass, 1977), pp. 50–52.

15. The nature and measurement of values has been a concern of anthropologists, philosophers, psychologists, sociologists, economists, social historians, and educators. No brief statement can encompass all the complexities and subtleties of the theorizing about values in all these disciplines. Our statement captures the central features of most definitions, a value being either a generalized preference or desire or else a generalized conception of the desirable—that is, of what one *ought* to desire. See, for example, Robin Williams, "The Concept of Values," in *International Encyclopedia of the Social Sciences* (New York: Macmillan, 1968), 16: 282–87; William K, Frankena, "Value and Valuation," in *Encyclopedia of Philosophy* (New York: Macmillan, 1967), 8: 229–32.

16. In his continuing program of research on changing American values, Yankelovich repeatedly asked a long battery of direct questions on *general* values in trend surveys conducted between 1968 and 1973. Whatever the limitations of such instruments, the data seem to provide a valuable source for special secondary analyses of enduring effects of education involving studies of trends or comparisons of values where the bias, assuming it were a constant, would not jeopardize such conclusions. But, as noted earlier, the surveys were limited to youth, aged sixteen to twenty-five, divided into two strata—those enrolled in college vs. those not in college—and thus provide no evidence on long-term effects among adults. See Daniel Yankelovich, *The New Morality: A Profile of American Youth in the 70's*, (New York: McGraw-Hill, 1974), chap. 6.

17. Rokeach has established that his instrument of this type yields reliable or stable measurements on retest but is also sensitive to real changes over time, and that it produces valid data as suggested by the differences obtained from contrasted groups of known character. See, for example, M. Rokeach, "Change and Stability in American Value Systems," *Public Opinion Quarterly* 38 (1974): 222–38. There are empirical as well as logical grounds for the view that such an instrument is not susceptible to response bias. Feather administered the Rokeach instrument to equivalent groups of Australian subjects under contrasted conditions: anonymity vs. signing one's name on the form. If there were a tendency to distort answers so as to present oneself in a more attractive light, it should be accentuated where one can be identified with his responses. The findings, almost without exception, were negative. See Norman T. Feather, *Values in Education and Society* (New York: Free Press, 1975), pp. 38–41.

18. Perhaps the earliest demonstration of this was in a 1940 Gallup Poll survey. To the question, "Do you believe in freedom of speech?" 97% answered yes. Those individuals were then asked, "Do you believe in it to the extent of allowing fascists and communists to hold meetings and express their views in this community?" to this 72% of the group who had initially endorsed the value answered no. See Hadley Cantril, *Gauging Public Opinion* (Princeton: Princeton University Press, 1944), p. 22.

141

19. Florian Znaniecki, whose classic writings from about 1910 onward brought the concept and study of values to prominence in sociology, also stresses the need to implicate specific situations in the instruments for the measurement of values. See his late work *Cultural Sciences: Their Origin and Development* (Urbana: University of Illinois Press, 1952), chap. 9.

20. Stephen B. Withey et al., *A Degree and What Else? Correlates and Consequences of a College Education* (New York: McGraw-Hill, 1972). Studies on the accuracy of voting reports as validated by official records show that some people who in fact cast ballots describe themselves as *not* having voted. Thus some of the error in measurement appears to be random in direction and simply a function of poor memory (since it is greater in reports about elections in the distant past) rather than a reflection of social desirability bias. In one validation study, Clausen arrived at a *generous* estimate that the magnitude of exaggeration in a national sample is about 8%. In a large-scale local survey in Denver, Cahalan found that the differences between educational groups in the *net* error in reports of voting in a series of elections averaged about 5%, and that both exaggerated claims and net errors were more characteristic of the *less* educated, making the observed findings conservative. Withey, however, found that the less educated were more likely to underreport voting, and the better educated to exaggerate voting, the two errors therefore working to make the difference between strata appear larger than it really is. However, the differences between strata in proneness to error (of either type) are very small in magnitude (see Withey's table 5). Aage Clausen, "Response Validity: Vote Report," *Public Opinion Quarterly* 32 (1968–69); 588–606, especially table 3; Don Cahalan, "Correlates of Respondent Accuracy in the Denver Validity Survey," *Public Opinion Quarterly* 32 (1968–69): 607–21, especially table 4.

21. Withey also reports that the college-educated show more political interest and are more likely to hold the kind of attitudes one would appraise as desirable; e.g., are less prejudiced about minorities, more tolerant, and so forth. Such opinion and attitude questions are not subject to the ambiguities surrounding conduct measures, and his overall conclusions about the good effects of college education must be given substantial weight.

22. Some other classic values could have been included in our study, since measures of them were available, but were deliberately omitted at the very beginning of our inquiry on grounds that their interpretation was bound to be ambiguous. For example, numerous questions in the surveys tapped religious values, a sphere covered in many standard tests of values. But it would be impossible to arrive at any consensus on whether education should inculcate religion, and the area was therefore omitted. Other values whose worth in the *abstract* would not have been difficult to appraise nevertheless have ambiguous meaning in any comparison of educational groups. Few would regard a desire for material things and comfort as an elevated value, and measures of the value were available. But if the more educated were found to place less emphasis on this value, it could not have been taken as evidence of good effects of education. As Rokeach has shown, the better educated, being better off, already have such comforts, whereas the uneducated, being poorer, understandably are still striving to reach that higher level of comfort. Therefore the test involves an unfair handicap.

23. As the reader will see, a discrete question sometimes was complex, containing subparts or subquestions. Nevertheless, it was counted as a "single" question, making the above total conservative.

24. One of the surveys we used, Stouffer's classic study of the erosion of the value of civil liberties during the McCarthy period, a highly controversial issue, was deliberately designed as two identical half-surveys, one conducted by the Gallup agency and the other by NORC, to test the insidious bias that might have arisen from the practices, staffing, and philosophy of either agency, despite the identical specifications for the in-

quiry. The Stouffer study is almost a unique instance of such a special safeguard built into the design of a single survey. Because it involves secondary analysis of many available surveys, it was possible to build this attractive feature into our design on a much larger scale.

25. J. P. Robinson et al., *Measures of Political Attitudes* (Ann Arbor, Mich.: Institute for Social Research, 1968), p. 591; Aage Clausen, "Response Validity," esp. pp. 598–602; Helen Dinerman, "1948 Votes in the Making"—A Preview," *Public Opinion Quarterly* 12 (1948): 590, note. In our earlier work, we checked the danger that reports of "having heard or read about an event" might be inflated because of the social desirability of appearing knowledgeable by reference to a subquestion testing actual knowledge of the events about which respondents had initially claimed awareness. The replicated finding in two surveys was that the more educated more frequently substantiated their claims of acquaintance. Since social desirability bias in these questions was more characteristic of the *less* educated, it worked to make the positive findings on effects of education compelling. *Enduring Effects of Education*, pp. 36–37, p. 126, table 2.

26. We may seem to be slighting the evidence from many methodological studies of social desirability bias. It is difficult to summarize that large and contradictory literature, but the following points seem crucial and faithful to those findings. Most of the studies are based on ad hoc samples of some subpopulation of college students, often answering questions in class or a lab for the benefit of a professor they know, often having to sign their names and at other times with no real protection of anonymity, and their answers relating to some obvious abnormality or unattractive quirk of personality. Generalizations from those kinds of samples of those specialized populations, those variables, and test conditions about the answers of adults in the usual sample survey involve a giant inferential leap. Since the academic studies are limited to college students, they establish that well-educated youth are prone to social desirability bias, but they can shed no light on whether the bias *varies by level of education*, or by age, the issues crucial to our research. A number of the methodological studies, however, do present more relevant evidence that should allay fear that social desirability bias will distort our survey findings. David Horton Smith incorporated a short form of the Crowne-Marlowe social desirability scale, an instrument designed to test the individual's predisposition to such bias, into a sample survey in Chile and computed the correlations between the social desirability score and answers to the ninety survey questions. Only *five* of the coefficients were significantly greater than zero ($r = .17$), at least two of these on questions dealing with most obvious virtues, and none exceeded .22. David Horton Smith, "Correcting for Social Desirability Response Sets in Opinion-Attitude Survey Research," *Public Opinion Quarterly* 31 (1967): 87–94. A battery of items from the Crowne-Marlowe test was incorporated into a survey of a national sample of youth. All the interitem correlations were less than .1, suggesting that social desirability bias is a very specific tendency, rather than a generalized trait of particular individuals or groups of individuals, and might distort the answers to particular types of questions and not others, even when all of them deal with desirable content. See J. P. Robinson and P. R. Shaver, *Measures of Social Psychological Attitudes* (Ann Arbor, Mich.: Institute for Social Research, 1969), pp. 661–62. For empirical evidence that social desirability bias does not distort measurements of personal values, even when couched in a general form, and for a telling critique of the idea that such biases are a major problem, see W. A. Scott, "Social Desirability and Individual Conceptions of the Desirable," *Journal of Abnormal and Social Psychology* 1963 (67): 574–85. In surveys where reports of "good" conduct, such as voting, have been validated, the evidence is that the difference between educational groups in false reports runs about 5% to 8%, with the *less* educated frequently being *more* prone to error. The findings that the educated are far more virtuous in these respects cannot be

accounted for by errors of such magnitude, and the direction of the error often works to make the findings more compelling. See Cahalan, "Correlates of Respondent Accuracy," especially table 4; Withey, *Degree*, esp. p. 8, table 5.

27. Nor should we neglect the amount of information about the quality of the questions obtained in the development stage of the original survey. One battery of questions we have used, originally appearing in the Stouffer study, had been through five pretests and revisions. "The semi-final pre-test involved interviews with 250 people at all educational levels in different parts of the United States and the final dress rehearsal was done on 50 persons also at different levels. Perhaps twice as many questions were tried out and discarded as appeared in the final questionnaire"; Samuel A. Stouffer, *Communism, Conformity, and Civil Liberties* (Garden City, N.Y.: Doubleday, 1955), p. 22. Consequently, as Stouffer notes (pp. 46–47), a good deal of evidence, both qualitative and quantitative, some based on interviewers' reports and some on tests in the course of analysis, suggests that there was almost complete candor and very little response error.

28. Given the dilemma the respondent confronts in many questions, it might seem that the most desirable posture would be to describe himself as "undecided." It turns out that a very small percentage of respondents answer in this fashion, and many or most of them must surely be conflicted rather than just posturing. The meaning of the undecided responses and their distribution by education will be treated later.

29. The careful reader will note that the battery of questions on abortion as used by NORC vs. Gallup varies the preface, the sequence in which the items are presented, and the specific wording of the items. The changes seem slight, but in subtle ways they could have powerful effects on the results. These variations provide a test of measurement errors, including "social desirability," which is made more salient by some of the subtle changes in wording.

30. Charles Herbert Stember, *Education and Attitude Change* (New York: Institute of Human Relations Press, 1961), p. 170.

31. Ibid., p. 27.

32. For the earliest period, see Herbert H. Hyman and Paul B. Sheatsley, "Trends in Public Opinion on Civil Liberties," *Journal of Social Issues* 9, no. 3 (1953): 6–16; Stouffer, *Communism, Conformity, and Civil Liberties*. For the later period see Hazel Erskine and Richard L. Siegel, "Civil Liberties and the American Public," *Journal of Social Issues* 31, no. 2 (1975): 13–29.

33. Herbert H. Hyman and Paul B. Sheatsley, "Attitudes on Desegregation," *Scientific American* 211, no 1 (July 1964): 2–9. Evidence is also presented here that such answers are not distorted by social desirability bias. See especially p. 5. For the later period, see Andrew M. Greeley and Paul B. Sheatsley, "Attitudes toward Racial Integration," *Scientific American* 225, no. 6 (December 1971): 13–19.

34. Stouffer, *Communism, Conformity, and Civil Liberties*, pp. 91–108; Hyman and Sheatsley, "Attitudes on Desegregation," especially pp. 8–9; James Davis, "Communism, Conformity, Cohorts, and Categories: American Tolerance in 1954 and 1972–73," *American Journal of Sociology* 81 (1975): 491–513.

35. The process clearly depends on the perception of the norm that prevails rather than on the true norm or the actual distribution in a population. There is a good deal of evidence of *pluralistic ignorance*, or inaccurate perception of the views of others, one common pattern being that individuals overrate the numbers who share their views and underestimate the numbers, often a large majority, who hold opposing views. This particular pattern of pluralistic ignorance would tend to reduce the social desirability bias that would occur even when a particular value has become widespread. On this particular pattern see Hubert O'Gorman, "Pluralistic Ignorance and White Estimates of White Support for Racial Segregation," *Public Opinion Quarterly* 39 (1975): 313–30; Hubert

O'Gorman with Stephen L. Garry, "Pluralistic Ignorance—A replication and Extension," *Public Opinion Quarterly* 40 (1976–77): 449–58.

36. The skeptic might question our assumption and argue that the educated would be more sensitive to the changing climate of opinion in the nation and that social desirability bias would therefore be of greater magnitude among them. He might cite the findings of our earlier study that the educated are more knowledgeable, more likely to use the media and to seek out current information, and reason therefore that they would be quicker to sense changing fashions in opinion. He might cite Stember's finding on prejudice that the educated are "considerably more labile than others, and more responsive to changing values and beliefs." Stember, *Education and Attitude Change*, p. 169. But the implications of these facts are not what they may seem and are anything but simple. If the argument is pushed, it cuts many ways. When the climate of national opinion is not monolithic, the educated would be more sensitive to how diverse the conceptions of the desirable are in different circles, and the net effect of social desirability bias would thus be *less* than among the uneducated. When the climate of opinion is monolithic and in the direction of "bad" values, the educated should be responsive, and any good effects would be conservatively stated, since they would feel pressure to suppress their real, better values. And if they are sensitive and labile, the consequences of any particular climate of opinion may be that their *true* opinions are altered, and not that they falsify their answers.

37. As the population moves closer to the ceiling or floor of the instrument in different time periods, problems also arise in assessing whether the effects of education persist, decline, or increase as a cohort ages, and are also solved by applying such indexes.

38. The technical details of the procedures employed in controlling these variables will be reviewed in chapters 2 and 3, along with the findings; but it should be noted that several different statistical approaches were used to insure sound conclusions about spuriousness.

39. In the course of their studies of long-term value changes among Dartmouth College graduates, Hoge and Bender provide evidence, albeit for only one college, on the historical change from the more highly selected, homogeneous student body of the past to the less selective and heterogeneous student body of recent times. The standard deviation of scores on the Allport-Vernon Study of Values is substantially larger on most of the value dimensions for the senior class of 1968 than for the senior class of 1940, studied twenty-eight years earlier. For example, on religious values, the SD increases over time from 6.57 to 8.98. The same pattern is demonstrated if one computes the coefficients of variation and takes into account the means of the distributions for the two classes. Hoge and Bender, *Factors Influencing Value Change*, p. 574, table 1. For more general evidence on such changes see Martin Trow, "The Second Transformation of American Secondary Education," *International Journal of Comparative Sociology* 2 (1961): 144–66.

40. For example, a ninth factor that has been found to influence educational attainment is number of siblings; individuals from *large* families are less likely to go far in school and college. The effect of this factor, however, has varied over time, been different for girls and for boys, and is due in part to the fact that large families have been more characteristic among rural, Catholic, and poor people, and in earlier generations. Thus this ninth factor is controlled in some degree by our controls on other social factors, and its influence can be examined by inspecting differential effects of education in our various social groups and cohorts. For the complex pattern of effects of family size on education, see Beverly Duncan, "Trends in Output and Distribution of Schooling," in *Indicators of Social Change*, ed. Eleanor Sheldon and Wilbert Moore (Russell Sage Foundation and Basic Books, 1968), pp. 645–48. Sheer family size, after it has been purified of its concomitants of residence, religion, and class by the controls on these factors, seems incon-

sequential for values. In studies of ordinal position, the effects of family size usually are separated out. There is some evidence that it affects affiliativeness or gregariousness and tendency to anxiety, as one might reasonably expect on social-psychological grounds, but even here the evidence is mixed and ambiguous, since controls for residence, class, and religion are rarely introduced, and such psychological phenomena are very different from the values we have studied. See, for example, Stanley Schachter, *The Psychology of Affiliation* (Stanford: Stanford University Press, 1959), pp. 53–57, especially the cautionary note on p. 55. As might be expected from parents who limit the number of their children (suggesting a desire to provide more of the benefits their money can buy for each member of the family), studies have documented that children from smaller families have higher intellectual achievement orientation, higher educational aspiration, higher academic performance, and—even when class is held constant—score higher on intelligence tests. These factors help account for the differences observed in educational attainment. However, as Clausen stresses in his careful review: "Family size, then, does appear to make a difference in the way children are reared and in the attributes they develop, but the effects are small and depend on a number of circumstances" (p. 14). And the differences documented pertain essentially to *intellectual* values rather than to the kinds of social values we are studying. See John A. Clausen, "Family Structure, Socialization, and Personality," in *Review of Child Development Research*, vol. 2, ed. Lois and Martin Hoffman (Russell Sage Foundation, 1966), pp. 1–53, especially pp. 9–15. In the course of Singer's large-scale study of ordinal position in the family, she documented that children from smaller families score higher on a scale of "adult orientation," but the relationship is different for boys and girls and for low- and high-status families and is not monotonic. Since the better-educated are more likely to come from small families, some of them, depending on sex, social class, and number of siblings, would have been more adult-oriented in some degree than their counterparts with less education. On this basis one might predict among specified subgroups of better educated that they would be likely to hold values *similar* to their parents' values, *whatever those might have been*, but this process could lead to a great variety of values. Eleanor Singer, "Adult Orientation of First and Later Children," *Sociometry* 34 (1971): 328–45.

41. In our earlier work, although one could assume from the late timing of the measurement of intelligence that it was an inflated estimate of the influence of IQ on education, the studies available provided no way of estimating how large that inflation was. A recent Swedish study by Fägerlind that provided measures of intelligence at age ten and again at age twenty after schooling establishes clearly that the inflation is substantial. After a careful review of this almost unique study, Bowman cautions us: "The strong path coefficients from education to ability in these Swedish data should make us wary of using measures of ability made *after* the schooling." Mary Jean Bowman, "Through Education to Earnings? A Review," *Proceedings of the National Academy of Education* 3 (1976): 221–92, especially p. 234. Earlier Swedish investigations, unknown to us at the time of our first study, also establish the influence of education on intelligence measured after various amounts of schooling. See K. Härnqvist, "Changes in Intelligence from 13 to 18," *Scandinavian Journal of Psychology* 9 (1968): 50–82; T. Husen, *Begävning och miljö* (Stockholm: Pettersons, 1951).

42. *Enduring Effects of Education*, pp. 25–29.

43. One cannot neglect the fact that even *particular* colleges that formerly tried to select only students with distinctive backgrounds and values have, as a matter of deliberate policy, tried in recent years to broaden their student bodies, and thus the variability in values among their freshmen has greatly increased. Compelling evidence is presented by Perry, who conducted intensive longitudinal studies of changes in ethical philosophy during the college years among students who entered Harvard in 1954, 1962, and 1963. "In the instance of Harvard College, the freshman class in 1900 consisted of 537 stu-

dents drawn from 175 schools. In 1960 the freshman class of 1082 was drawn from 499 schools. In 1900, 45 percent of entering students came from outside Massachusetts; in 1960, 72 percent. It could hardly be said any longer, as Adams had said of his classmates in the 1850s, that the students had nothing to give each other because they had been 'brought up together under like conditions.' " William G. Perry, Jr., *Forms of Intellectual and Ethical Development in the College Years* (New York: Holt, Rinehart and Winston, 1970), p. 6. Therefore, if our positive findings on the effects of education were spurious, simply a reflection of initial differences in values, they should decline markedly in our recent surveys and cohorts, which as the reader will soon see, is not the case.

44. Peter Rose, "The Myth of Unanimity: Student Opinions on Critical Issues," *Sociology of Education* 37 (1963): 142. Another study of thirteen small colleges documents the great variability in the support of civil liberties among the freshmen entering in 1955. See Arthur Chickering, "Civil Liberties and the Experience of College," *Journal of Higher Education*, vol. 41 (1970): especially pp. 600–601.

45. Feldman and Newcomb, *Impact of College*, pp. 40, 45, 52, 99.

46. Alan E. Bayer et al., "The First Year of College: A Follow-up Normative Report," *ACE Research Reports* 5, no. 1 (February 1970): 33. In computing these ranges, we excluded the freshmen in a fifth type of institution, "predominantly Negro colleges" to make the finding on variability applicable to the all-white population included in our studies.

47. *Enduring Effects of Education*, pp. 29–30.

Chapter 2 The Findings

1. *Enduring Effects of Education*, p. 299, n. 1.

2. Those who were coded "no answer" are omitted from all analyses, representing error by the interviewer, mainly in omitting to ask the question.

3. Jean Converse has recently reported a thorough analysis of the magnitude, distribution by education, and other correlates of the "don't know" response to some three hundred questions of widely varied content and format asked in Gallup and Harris surveys. Although she *generally* finds a significant and substantial difference by education, the "don't know" response being more common among the *less* educated, it should be stressed that on questions similar in content to ours—on morality and crime, for example —the percentage undecided of the national sample is very low, and "the evidence from the Gallup questions is that most people appear to have opinions on those matters of traditional belief . . . and in fact the grade-school-educated are quite as well equipped to answer such questions as the college educated, for the mean difference in the No Opinion of these two groups is only 1 percent to 3 percent on these topics" (p. 527). Jean Converse, "Predicting No Opinion in the Polls," *Public Opinion Quarterly* 40 (1976): 515–30.

4. The p values presented are those for a two-tailed test, which also tends to make conclusions about the effects of education conservative.

5. The sign of the gamma, of course, depends on which way variables are arranged spatially in the matrix—whether the "good" or "high" end is positioned to left or right or top or bottom. The variables have always been arranged so that a positive sign denotes an increase in the "*good*" value with more education. Occasional apparent contradictions between the pattern the reader observes in the first three columns and the sign and magnitude of the gamma arise because the gamma and the chi-square are computed over all the five or *six* refined levels of education rather than just from the *three* groups of graduates. The pattern may become stronger or weaker or reversed when all levels are taken into account. Using many levels of education and many cells to compute chi-square and gamma tends to reduce the coefficient and to make the picture of the effects

and their significance even more conservative. See our earlier work. *Enduring Effects of Education*, p. 300, n. 4.

6. The complete instrument (see Appendix A) involved the respondent's judging which *one* was the most desirable of all, thereafter judging which three were least important, and finally judging which one was least important of all. Since it would be impossible to obtain consensus on which single trait was the very best and which the worst, our analysis is based only on classifying the seven traits into: among the three best, among the three worst, and among neither the best nor the worst. The six qualities eliminated from our analysis are ambiguous criterion measures. Some judges would regard them as highly desirable and others as less desirable. Obedience and striving for success are two examples. The original instrument was developed by Melvin Kohn on the basis of intensive interviews and a community survey, then it was simplified and reduced to its present form for his national survey in 1964. Since that survey was restricted to a sample of employed males, and the questions were asked only of fathers, who were instructed to answer in terms of one of their own children, specified by age and sex, we could not use the 1964 survey data as a baseline from an earlier time period. See Melvin Kohn, *Class and Conformity: A Study in Values* (Homewood, Ill.: Dorsey Press, 1969).

7. Our earlier study provided strong, though indirect, evidence that the educated do value the intellect. They were more receptive than the lesser educated to current information, more likely to seek it out and to expose themselves to print media. They clearly exhibit greater intellectual curiosity than the less educated. *Enduring Effects of Education*, passim. This in no way contradicts the new finding that the more educated do not unduly elevate intellectual values to top rank in their *hierarchy* of values. The two sets of findings taken together suggest that education has created an appreciation of the intellect without producing an exaggerated sense of its relative importance.

8. Another item in the original battery was "being a good student." This was not included in our cluster of "intellectual values," since Kohn had established by factor analysis and other evidence that it essentially indicates the value of *conformity to authority*. By these same modes of analysis, Kohn found that honesty has different factor loadings in the middle and lower classes, and he concluded that it has a complex and dual meaning. It is sometimes indicative of a moral value or internal standard of proper conduct but, surprisingly, sometimes indicates an instrumental orientation, honesty being an avenue to popularity and success. The complexity of meaning may also account for our mixed and confusing finding. Kohn, *Class and Conformity*, passim.

9. Kohn, however, found that better-educated parents, even when social class was controlled, were more likely to give high rank to the moral value of consideration for others. Kohn, *Class and Conformity*, p. 31.

10. The reader will observe from the detailed wordings in Appendix A that some of the questions specify the content of the communication and others only the character of the communicator.

11. These examples of the specific questions used as indicators of values may suggest to the sociological theorist that our study deals with the effects of education on *norms* rather than on *values*, a valid conceptual distinction. In Robin Williams's phrasing, "Norms . . . say more or less specifically what should or should not be done by particular types of actors in given circumstances. Values are standards of desirability that are more nearly independent of specific situations . . . a particular norm may represent the simultaneous application of several separable values." But, as he notes, depending on the level of generality, a point can be reached where norm "becomes practically indistinguishable from value." For all the methodological reasons noted earlier, we preferred to use highly specific questions, indicators of norms if one so regards them; but by using a wide range of such items one can, as he puts it, "disentangle the generalized value principle from

the admixture of other values and other determinants of behavior." Williams, "Concept of Values," pp. 284–85.

12. The 1954 Stouffer survey from which these data are drawn was one of the very few surveys where the original codes were such that the four age-groupings we use had to depart from our standard practice. Although the cutting points are rather similar and do not impair study of regressions with age, the reader should keep this in mind in making comparisons with findings elsewhere in table C.2.1 and later tables. It should be noted that in table C.2.1 we have used only the *NORC half* of the Stouffer study in order to maintain comparability with the NORC survey data for the later periods.

13. In his original analyses of these data Stouffer presents persuasive, though not definitive, evidence that some of the apparent decline with aging simply reflects special rearing and educational practices to which this particular generation was exposed. Stouffer, *Communism, Conformity, and Civil Liberties*, pp. 94–100.

14. The question dealing with the communist teacher asks specifically whether he should be "fired," whereas the other questions ask only whether the nonconformist should be allowed to teach. The usage "fired" is more extreme and makes that particular finding even more compelling. A battery of questions to document nationwide trends in support of civil liberties in the 1970s was included in surveys conducted by the Response Analysis Corporation in 1970, 1971, and 1975. Comparison of two of the items confirms, at the aggregate level, the pattern of relatively strong opposition to the atheist. In all three surveys, the percentage answering "yes" to the question, "Should people be allowed to make speeches against God?" was *smaller* than to the question, "Should people be allowed to publish books which attack our system of government?" *Sampler* (Princeton: Response Analysis Corporation), spring 1977, no. 8, p. 4.

15. Differentiation in applying the values could have been examined in a less qualitative and more formal statistical fashion, for example, by computing separate interitem correlation matrices for each of the educational levels and age-groups, leading to conclusions about the degree to which various groups integrate their specific views into a thoroughly consistent, generalized system of ideas about liberty. These procedures were not employed, partly because of the laboriousness and expense in computing all these statistics for all the matrices and also because the intercorrelations would only convey the consistent ranking of individuals and not whether there were changes in magnitude of support for the value in different situations. More important, judges would not arrive at the same verdict after reviewing such findings, and all the labor would have been for naught. Some judges would wish that all individuals, especially the more educated, would thoughtfully weigh the circumstances in which the value should be applied and make sharp discriminations. Other judges might argue that the educated ought to show an undifferentiated and global support of liberty under all the conditions involved. What exact balance between differentiation and integration of facets of this value system is ideal remains undecided.

16. Items 16 and 17 were also asked in another national survey (#401) conducted by NORC in January 1957. For reasons of economy, this survey was excluded from our data set and detailed analyses, but the published basic results clearly show that the aggregate measurements are very stable across the two 1957 surveys.

17. The data, in table C.2.3, are presented in terms of the four standard age categories, whereas in table C.2.1, because of the original codes in the Stouffer 1954 survey, the age-categories had to be slightly different. The definition of the elementary-school group is not the same in both periods. This incomparability should not affect the basic conclusions about the effects of different cycles of education on contrasted generations, and it will be eliminated in the later refined analyses.

18. Our findings for the 1970s, derived from the 1972 and 1974 NORC surveys, are dramatically confirmed in a recent report of a third nationwide survey, conducted in 1973 by a different agency, the Response Analysis Corporation. The score on a scale composed of our items 1–9 plus six additional items, all fifteen drawn from Stouffer's original 1954 study, is indicative of the level of overall "tolerance" or general support of civil liberties for nonconformists. Within each of five age cohorts, such support increased monotonically with each increment of education, and the effects were strong. For example, among those aged sixty or older, 65% of the college graduates score at the more tolerant end of the scale, whereas only 14% of those with a grade-school education receive such a score. But, as in our analysis, at each level of education, tolerance declines with age. Clyde Z. Nunn, Harry J. Crockett, Jr., and J. Allen Williams, Jr., *Tolerance for Nonconformity* (San Francisco: Jossey-Bass, 1978), pp. 81–82.

19. When the reader juxtaposes the summary findings in tables C.2.1 and C.2.3, he also sees vividly the dramatic changes in the nationwide climate of opinion since the 1950s. In the 1970s, in every age-group and educational level within it, support of civil liberties is far more prevalent than in the corresponding cell in the 1950s. As we remarked before and as we shall stress again, the context of the times is constant and in no way jeopardizes comparisons between educational levels and age-groups at any one point in time. The conclusions for the different time periods, in turn, can be compared to see whether there are uniformities in the educational effects and in the aging process that transcend the particular period.

20. In the last pair of comparisons, the reader will note the slight departure from comparability. Because of the original codes, the oldest group in 1954 had to be defined as sixty or over. By defining the oldest group in 1974 as sixty to sixty-nine, various advantages accrued; this minor change, leaving out the small number over seventy, cannot have had much effect on the conclusion.

21. For a thoughtful treatment of the various meanings of floor and ceiling effects, of the dangers of applying corrections mechanically, and of appropriate transformations and their properties, see Norval Glenn, *Cohort Analysis*, Sage University Paper Series on Quantitative Applications in the Social Sciences (Beverly Hills, Calif.: Sage Publications, 1977), pp. 64–68.

22. Note that the earlier question referred to "prisoners"—*convicted* or proved criminals—whereas this pair of questions deals with those who are *suspected* of crimes, but not yet proved criminals. In supporting the rights of the latter group but not the former group, some judges would say that the educated make a proper and important distinction, and they would therefore regard the earlier finding as no flaw at all in the pattern of good effects of education.

23. In close to half the tests where religion was controlled, the variable measured in the original survey was the respondent's religion during *childhood*. That this variable is antecedent to education and might also have determined the individual's later values was ideally suited to our needs. However, in the other surveys in our set, the variable measured was the *current* religious affiliation of the adult, which perforce was used as the best approximation to the antecedent factor. As noted in our earlier work, the slippage between the ideal variable and the one we actually measured and employed in these instances is of trivial consequence, since the proportion of white adults who had changed from their childhood affiliations as Protestants and Catholics in these periods is only about 3%. *Enduring Effects of Education*, p. 302, n. 1. In most of the tests where social-class origin was controlled, the classification is based on questions about *both* the mother's and the father's education, "high" in these tests defined as having at least one parent who had some college education and "low" including all cases where both parents had between nine and twelve years of school or else one parent did, the other parent not having gone beyond eighth grade, so as to serve our need to create relatively homoge-

neous groups that were of substantial size. In other surveys, social-class origin is based on father's occupation, those in the "high" category coming from professional or managerial backgrounds and those in the "low" from blue-collar backgrounds.

24. In the 1970 samples in the aggregate, for whites aged twenty-five to seventy-two, about 97% were native-born. Among the three cohorts, aged twenty-five to thirty-six, thirty-seven to forty-eight, and forty-nine to sixty, the percentage native-born varies slightly. Using one of our 1974 surveys for estimates, the foreign-born number 2%, 2%, and 4% respectively. Given the negligible number of immigrants, any refinements in the conceptualization and control of the variable become trivial and academic. Obviously, *age at time of immigration* is the proper measure of whether one's education was obtained outside the United States, is also central to understanding what societal values were learned in the course of socialization, and must be considered for full understanding of the general reduction in educational attainment found among immigrants. For a recent reexamination and revision of theory on this last process, see Michael Inbar, *The Vulnerable Age Phenomenon*, Occasional Publications Reviewing New Fields for Social Science Development no. 8, (New York: Russell Sage Foundation, 1976).

25. In Stouffer's original 1954 inquiry, controls on current residential location (simultaneously controlling region and size of community), sex (simultaneously controlling region and/or size of community), and religious orthodoxy showed that the educational differences on the overall scale score (a composite of the items we used) persisted. His findings are consonant with our findings from the controlled tests for that period and later periods. Stouffer, *Communism, Conformity, and Civil Liberties*, pp. 120–21, 134–35, 146. In their 1973 survey, Nunn, Crockett, and Williams also show that the educational differences in overall scale scores persist when sex is controlled and that the effects are just as great in magnitude after the control is introduced as they were before the control. *Tolerance for Nonconformity*, p. 115, table 45, p. 60, table 14.

26. Nunn, Crockett, and Williams show that the educational differences in overall scale scores on tolerance persist when current occupation is controlled, not only in their "white-collar" group but also in their "blue-collar" group. That they observed no weakening of effects among those who ended up in lower occupations, whereas we did, may simply reflect differences in the procedures they applied to this one particular test. Their cutting points for education were different, and since their operational definition of "blue collar" is not specified, that also may have differed. *Tolerance for Nonconformity*, p. 62, table 15.

27. See Appendix A for the full wording. We have added the emphasis to make clear the general audience involved and to show that the issue is not making available birth-control devices, but only the information about birth control.

28. Since a considerable number of Catholics, albeit a small minority, attended parochial schools, that might have contributed to the differential and occasional inverse effects observed and have been in the spirit of the goals of those educational institutions. For estimates of the frequency of parochial schooling, see our earlier work. *Enduring Effects of Education*, p. 65, p. 303, n. 2.

29. Respondents, of course, do not always respond to the niceties of a question, and some might argue that on this question they missed the distinctions we have noted and are simply expressing their preferences or prejudices about intermarriage. There is little foundation for the argument in this instance. From Stember's encyclopedic secondary analysis of prejudice, we know that fewer than 10% of whites, about 1960, approved of white-black intermarriage, whereas the reader will soon see from our table that almost 50% of all whites about the same time *opposed* laws to prevent intermarriage. Clearly, a large number of individuals are not simply expressing their own prejudices when they answer our question. What they would not do or approve of themselves, they do not wish to deny to others through such laws. Moreover, Stember finds very little relation between

such personal preferences and education and in one instance reports a *negative* relationship, whereas we shall report strong positive relationships. Our question, fairly, may be regarded as dealing with the value of freedom and its protection from the constraint of law. See Stember, *Education and Attitude Change*, pp. 131–32.

30. As Appendix A indicates, the three replicated tests in the early 1950s are based on the very same question. The version used in the late 1960s is somewhat different, and the version used in the 1970s, though identical in the replicated tests, is different from that in the earlier two periods. The consistency of the findings from these different versions shows how stable the pattern is. However, no matter what the precise wording, in all the surveys an initial filter question eliminated respondents who reported that they had no knowledge or idea at all about the nature of wiretapping. After this screening process, only those with at least some rudimentary knowledge or conception of wiretapping were left for the subsequent analysis, and the usual effects of education may have been dampened. Although this might have contributed to the negligible effects observed, it seems unlikely that it could account for the *inverse* effects we shall present.

31. For such evidence, see also, Erskine and Siegel, "Civil Liberties and the American Public," p. 24.

32. That technical problems of ceiling influence these particular findings is suggested by various facts. In most of the comparisons prevalence increases by about 20 percentage points, but where a particular cohort starts from a rather low baseline, the increase is much larger. A national survey conducted in 1944 (and therefore outside the scope of our study), a time when such values were far less pervasive in the population, had used the identical question on job equality and therefore can test for effects under conditions where the low ceiling is eliminated. Stember analyzed the evidence on effects for that generation, educated about twenty years earlier than the cohorts measured in our 1963 survey, and showed that prevalence of the value increased by about 30 percentage points. Stember, *Education and Attitude Change*, p. 73. Large educational differences were also documented in a 1946 survey that used the identical question. See Hazel Erskine, "The Polls: Negro Employment," *Public Opinion Quarterly* 32 (1968): 139.

33. The effect of education in these other areas of prejudice and race relations is indeed an important problem, and the positive findings add greatly to the credit of education, but Stember has already provided elaborate evidence of the good effects in many, though not all, of these areas, and our study was specifically focused on effects on values.

34. Stember, *Education and Attitude Change*, pp. 60–61.

35. Since the truncated samples shrank so much after these exclusions, we had to use a grosser breakdown into two age-groups. If we had used the standard four age-groups, some of the cells would have been too small to warrant any conclusions. This is not to suggest that all women use that membership group as a reference group or regard a woman president as serving their interests. (The same point could be made about Catholics, etc.) Indeed, the finding from trend analyses, paradoxically, was that during the 1960s men were *more favorable* than women to a woman presidential candidate. See Hazel Erskine, "The Polls: Women's Role," *Public Opinion Quarterly* 35 (1971): 275–90. However, by confining our analyses to males, we surely control the variable of group interest, thus reducing a good deal of the complexity, still not fully understood, that has been found in the patterns and trends in female support for a woman president and that might confound our conclusions. On these fascinating but somewhat mysterious complexities, see Myra Ferree, "A Woman for President?" *Public Opinion Quarterly* 38 (1974): 390–99.

36. Only one survey in our set of thirty-eight included this battery for the 1950s. But there was no need to strain our resources and add other surveys. Our evidence for that period on this particular value is confirmed by Stember's analyses of the very same questions in two surveys conducted in 1952 and 1958. Education increased support for a

black or a Jewish candidate in both surveys. *Education and Attitude Change*, pp. 61–62, 76.

37. Juxtaposing these findings on *voting* for an atheist with the earlier finding on whether an atheist should be *allowed to hold public office* (see table C.2.2) again suggests the special and demanding character of the questions measuring equality of political opportunity. Although a majority of the people denied the atheist the right to hold public office, in every age and educational group (with one exception), the proportion who would themselves vote for the atheist candidate for president is much smaller than the proportion who would allow him to hold public office. Education also has much less effect on the voting question.

38. The combined test of the effects of education on support for a black candidate for those aged sixty-one to seventy-two would be significant, leaving only one instance where the results for the very old would be nonsignificant.

39. By separate multiple regression analyses of the 1958 and 1967 surveys, incorporating the variables of age, religion, region, size of community, and party affiliation, Ferree also concludes that "it is particularly striking how little education predicted willingness to vote for a woman" "Ferree, "A Woman for President?" p. 395.

40. The length of the battery varied, however. The atheist question interrupted the sequence in one of our surveys, and other items we did not use—e.g., a Baptist candidate —interrupted the sequence in various of the surveys.

41. There is an obvious hypothesis about the incongruity in the findings. The analysis presented for the woman candidate only examined the effects of education among *men*, whereas the other three questions examined the effects of education for *both* men and women together. However, separate runs for *men* show that education has positive effects on the other three questions of the same magnitude, as was shown in the tables for the two sexes together.

42. The question on the black candidate in *one* of the surveys was preceded by questions on the busing of Negro and white children, on school integration, and on interracial marriage that may have influenced the subsequent answers and made them less comparable to the Gallup finding and to the replicated finding in the other NORC survey.

43. Ferree had used the NORC 1972 survey in her analysis and reported small but positive effects of education on male support for a woman candidate. This may have added to the instability and mystery surrounding these data, but when combined with our findings from the two other NORC surveys they may have swung the overall conclusion toward some modest effects emerging in the recent period. Ferree, "A Woman for President?", Table 3, p. 396.

44. Further evidence of the validity of these items, reminiscent of the classic method of using known criterion groups to establish the validity of an instrument, is provided in a study of southern cultural patterns. There is a great deal of evidence that southerners, predominantly Protestant, place greater emphasis on religion than northerners; that they exhibit, in Reed's phrase, "sectarianism and religious xenophobia." Consequently, if our questions on voting for an atheist, Catholic, or Jew have validity they should discriminate sharply between southerners and northerners, the southerners being much more likely to oppose such individuals. Reed presents these comparisons, repeating them four times for the Jewish and Catholic candidates from the surveys available and once for the atheist from the only such survey available. The differences between South and North, even with multiple controls on other demographic factors, are sharp and consistent, and in the direction to be expected if the items are valid. See John S. Reed, *The Enduring South* (Lexington, Mass.: D.C. Heath, 1972), pp. 64–65, 76–77.

45. In his analyses of these same measures of social, economic, and political equality in surveys from an earlier period, Stember also finds that the educational differences generally persist despite the introduction of multiple controls, thus strengthening our con-

clusion that the effects are not spurious. Stember, *Education and Attitude Change*, chap. 3.

46. The wordings NORC used in the 1970 surveys (see Appendix A) introduce the modifiers that the mother's health would be "seriously" endangered and that there was a "strong chance" of "serious" defect in the baby. The gravity of the dangers is thereby emphasized as well as the greater likelihood of occurrence. These changes might have contributed in some unknown degree to the trend toward increasing support.

47. The NORC wording in the 1970s is a bit more emphatic, stating that the "family has a *very low income* and cannot afford any more children," and the change in wording might have had some minor effect.

48. Two other Gallup surveys conducted in 1968 contained the battery of items 1–3 but were excluded from our data set and detailed analyses for reasons of economy. However, Judith Blake's findings reveal the same pattern as in the other surveys. For white non-Catholics, opposition to the legalization of abortion in each of the three circumstances is more characteristic of the *less* educated, and the finding holds when sex is controlled. See Judith Blake, "Abortion and Public Opinion: The 1960–1970 Decade," *Science* 171 (February 1971): 540–49, especially tables 2, 3, and 4.

49. NORC used a similar item in the 1970s, employed in our analyses of the effect of education during that period. However, the wording is less emphatic (see Appendix A), not explicitly stating that the financial status and health of the mother were no hindrance to having the child. The question, in contrast to the Gallup sequence, was asked before the questions on financial stress and dangers to the health of the mother, and respondents may have assumed that these factors were among the reasons the mother did not want another child. By comparing Gallup and NORC findings in the 1970s, Blake establishes that these procedural factors affect the findings on *aggregate* approval, but this in no way impairs our comparisons among educational groups. Blake also documents, in the course of these analyses, the high reliability of the findings when either of the questions is used in repeated surveys. See Judith Blake, "The Supreme Court's Abortion Decisions and Public Opinion in the United States," *Population and Development Review*, vol. 3, nos. 1–2 (1977), especially pp. 48–49.

50. When these analyses are made separately for Protestants and Catholics, the same differential effects are obtained as with items 1–3. Among Protestants the effects are substantial and significant. Among Catholics the effects are markedly dampened, in no instance significant, and in one test the effects are inverse, the gamma having a negative sign.

51. Although we have no way of subjecting these to empirical testing, several hypotheses about the decline with age in support on particular items may be suggested. One may be a loss of *sympathetic identification* with the circumstances of the individuals involved. It is surely harder for a person in her sixties to imagine herself in the position of a young unwed mother than it is for a younger respondent. The anomalous pattern observed in which the old and the educated both show little, or perhaps even less, support for the *poor* family's alleviating its burdens through legal abortion may also represent their lesser ability to identify with this plight because of their own better circumstances. It takes some time for education to produce an economic payoff, and the payoff was greater in earlier periods. Therefore the particular educational groups in our table—from older and earlier generations—who show the anomalous pattern would be further removed economically from the plight of the poor. For evidence on changing economic returns from education, see Richard Freeman, *The Declining Economic Value of Higher Education and the American Social System* (Aspen Institute, 1976) especially table 2, p. 4. Another possibility is that with advanced age "life becomes more precious" and protecting it simply takes precedence over the gains to be derived from the abortion in circumstances 3–5. The aged have also lived through many crises and thus realize that these pass and that one survives and manages despite adversity. The reasons for legalizing

abortion may therefore seem less compelling to them. For still other hypotheses, see Blake, "The Supreme Court's Abortion Decisions," passim.

52. For a summary of survey data f.om 1936 to 1969, see Hazel Erskine, "The Polls: Capital Punishment," *Public Opinion Quarterly* 34 (1970): 290–307.

53. See Appendix A for the various versions.

54. Schuman and Presser conducted an experiment in which two sharply different versions of the question on gun control were administered to equivalent subsamples in a 1975 national survey, and replicated it in a 1976 survey. The stability of the findings despite the radical change in wording shows that these views are highly crystallized. They also confirm from both surveys and both wordings that education and support of gun registration have little relationship. Howard Schuman and Stanley Presser, "Attitude Measurement and the Gun Control Paradox," *Public Opinion Quarterly* 41 (1977): 427–38.

Chapter 3   Conclusion

1. Not to burden the reader, in the text we have presented the findings from only one of the modes employed for controlling such factors. That evidence, based on partial contingency tables, had the advantage of showing not only the effects of education in subgroups matched on some other factor—for example, social-class origins—and thus controlling that source of spurious conclusions, but also of testing whether the effects of education were differential and contingent upon some other factor, for example, middle-class origin. But we also employed other conventional statistical methods of control, not presented in the text, that were equivalent to partial correlation techniques. To cite illustrative findings for the variable of social-class origins, usually regarded as so weighty a factor in accounting for selective educational attainment, the zero-order gamma expressing the relation between education (over its full range) and the eighteen items in the 1970s on civil liberties (from the Stouffer scale carried on the 1972 and 1974 surveys) had an average value of .46. The partial gamma, after controlling the variable social origins, had an average value of .41, showing that generally this factor (indexed by a combination of mother's and father's education) made hardly any contribution to our original finding. This agrees well with the refined findings based on partial contingency tables presented in table D.1. These two different approaches to controlling *other* sources of spuriousness also agreed. The reduction in the effects of education shown after controlling social origins, no matter by which method and no matter how small that reduction was, may nevertheless discount education too much. In the course of his thorough reexamination and comprehensive conceptualization of the evidence in his chapter "The Individual and Social Value of American Higher Education," Bowen presents a neglected and rather startling, but persuasive, reformulation of the conclusions to be drawn from such controlled tests. Since he is arguing against strongly entrenched, if questionable, ideas, we quote him at some length. "One of the most important outcomes of higher education is the favorable effect of parents' education on the intelligence and achievement of children. . . . This intergenerational transmission of higher education means that the effect on the generation receiving the education is augmented by its subsequent effect on later generations, and that estimates of the consequences for a single generation substantially understate the total impact of given increments of education. The intergenerational consequences of higher education may also be considered in reverse. In most studies of educational outcomes, much attention is given to distinguishing the effect of the current generation's education from the effects of their socioeconomic background. But when socioeconomic background is seen as partly the effect of education received in the past by parents, grandparents, and even more distant ancestors, then some part of socioeconomic background must be ascribed to education. The abilities and achievements of

the present generation are seen partly as a result of their own education and partly as a result of education received by their ancestors. When socioeconomic background is not properly taken into account, *the error is not necessarily overstating the effect of education* but rather failing to distinguish between education that occurred earlier and education that occurred later" (pp. 198–99, our italics). Howard Bowen, *Investment in Learning: The Individual and Social Value of American Higher Education* (San Francisco: Jossey-Bass, 1977). We also remind the reader that our design, as reviewed in chapter 1, provided *indirect* control over various factors that might otherwise have been sources of spurious conclusions.

2. Erskine and Siegel, *Civil Liberties.*

3. Stouffer, *Communism, Conformity, and Civil Liberties*; Hyman and Sheatsley, *Attitudes on Desegregation*; Angus Campbell, *White Attitudes toward Black People* (Ann Arbor: Institute for Social Research, 1971); Gertrude J. Selznick and Stephen Steinberg, *The Tenacity of Prejudice: Anti-Semitism in Contemporary America* (New York: Harper Torchbooks, 1969), p. 169; Gabriel A. Almond and Sidney Verba, *The Civic Culture* (Princeton: Princeton University Press, 1963), passim; Bowen, *Investment in Learning*, part 2. Stephens and Long cite additional evidence from the news releases and published reports of five other national surveys showing a *negative* correlation between years of schooling and racial prejudice. This evidence, combined with a much larger body of evidence collated from studies of students and various other specialized populations and then carefully reviewed, led them to conclude that "schooling exerts a broad, general influence on a variety of political behavior variables—*political tolerance* ... lack of *prejudice.*" And after examining the patterns they conclude that it is not just the effects of college, but that "high school also appears to make a difference." William N. Stephens and C. Stephen Long, "Education and Political Behavior," in *Political Science Annual: An International Review*, ed. James A. Robinson (Indianapolis: Bobbs-Merrill, 1970), pp. 3–33, especially pp. 7–8, 15. Inglehart's path analysis of pooled data from national surveys conducted in five *European* countries in 1971 provides powerful evidence that education contributes to "post-materialist" (in contrast with materialistic) values, after social-class origins and age are statistically controlled. His analysis of American survey data, though not as carefully controlled, also reveals positive effects. See Ronald Inglehart, *The Silent Revolution: Changing Values and Political Styles among Western Publics* (Princeton: Princeton University Press, 1977), especially pp. 84–89.

4. *Enduring Effects of Education*, pp. 117–18.

5. Models that can be fruitfully followed in designing research into this array of problems are plentiful in the literature. For an intensive longitudinal study of the process of formation and change of ethical value systems during four years of college, see, for example, William G. Perry, Jr., *Forms of Intellectual and Ethical Development in the College Years* (New York: Holt, Rinehart and Winston, 1970). For a design that traces the maintenance or erosion in adult life of the earlier changes produced by college education, see Theodore M. Newcomb et al., *Persistence and Change: Bennington College and Its Students after Twenty-five Years* (New York: John Wiley, 1967). For a design that analyzes the maintenance of earlier changes despite a hostile environment in terms of reference groups, see Herbert H. Hyman, Charles R. Wright, and Terence K. Hopkins, *Applications of Methods of Evaluation* (Berkeley: University of California Press, 1962). It is ironic that some investigators, attracted by such models, have recommended or employed longitudinal designs without control groups to obtain generalizable evidence on the magnitude of the effects of education. Such designs cannot serve that purpose (see note 3 to chapter 1 for some of the limitations). Their appropriate point of application comes after the magnitude of effects has been established by very different designs, such as the one we employed in our current study.

6. The "index of effectiveness" employed routinely in the first study, and occasionally in this study, expresses the gain with education relative to the maximum gain possible given the baseline on the item. This device enabled us to take into account difficulty in comparing a variety of effects. It was used in both studies for comparisons of the same or similar items between periods, but we hesitate to apply it across such different domains. Even within domains, our discussion on pp. 83–84 and on pp. 54–55 of our earlier work suggests that the meaning of the index is ambiguous.

7. R. M. Hare, "Adolescents into Adults," in *Moral Education*, ed. Barry I. Chazan and Jonas F. Soltis (New York: Teachers College Press, 1974), p. 117.

8. George S. Counts, *Dare the Schools Build a New Social Order,* the John Day Pamphlets, no. 11 (New York: John Day, 1932), p. 10.

9. Ibid., p. 12.

10. Hare, in Chazan and Soltis, *Moral Education*, p. 119. Examination of the other essays in this fine recent collection of readings on moral education, beginning with G. E. Moore's "The Indefinability of Good," provides additional evidence for our assertion. A recent critique of the methods and materials for moral education developed by Sidney Simon and Lawrence Kohlberg, two of the current prestigious figures in the field, vividly conveys how much confusion, doubt, and even opposition would be aroused in the thoughtful teacher who entertained their approaches, and how little effect they might have. See William J. Bennett and Edwin J. Delattre, "Moral Education in the Schools," *Public Interest*, no. 50 (winter 1978), pp. 81–98.

11. Lawrence A. Cremin, *Public Education* (New York: Basic Books, 1976), p. 36; our italics.

12. Ibid., p. 62.

13. Cremin, *Public Education*, p. 47.

Name Index